CU00239705

Studies in Prophecy

by Arno Clemens Gaebelein

FOREWORD.

BY C. I. SCOFIELD.

The present interest in prophetical studies, due to a world-situation so unprecedented as to have no historic parallels upon which a shallow optimism may build futile hopes, is in every way to be welcomed and encouraged. It surely is a divine provision for such a day as this that for the last fifty years the prophetic word has been under the sane and patient study of so many men of devout and trained minds. Amongst these the author of this book has won a foremost place. At the farthest possible remove from fanciful and radical methods of interpretation, the conclusions which he has reached and which are set forth in this book are trustworthy. The reader may be assured that he will reach truly Biblical views of those things which are coming to pass with startling rapidity.

Douglaston, L. I., N. Y.

"STUDIES IN PROPHECY"

THE PRESENT AGE: ITS BEGINNING, PROGRESS AND END
Ecclesiastes i:9

The Book of Ecclesiastes is the Book in which the natural man speaks. The conclusion which the wisest man reached is that all is vanity, and there is nothing new under the sun. In this first chapter we read of generations which come and go. The sun rises and goes down; the wind goeth toward the south, and turneth about to the north again, according to its circuits. The rivers go into the sea, and to the place where they come from they again return. All moves in nature in cycles. What has been is always to be again, and what was done will be done again.

This is likewise true in respect to God's dealings with man and with the earth. That which has been shall be; and what was done will be done again.

The future will repeat the past,
As the first, shall be the last;
Ages of change between.

Once the earth was undefiled by sin. It was the Paradise of God. For a brief period it knew no sorrow, no suffering, no curse and no death. That is what has been; but it shall surely be again. Creation will have a second birth, and after its travail pains, death and the curse will flee away. Once peace reigned, no strife was known and no groans heard in all creation's realm. That is what has been; it shall be so again. Groaning creation will be delivered; peace on earth and glory to God in the highest will follow.

Once man, the first man, unfallen, reigned. All things were under his feet. That has been before sin stripped man of his inheritance. But what has been, is that which shall be. The second man, the last Adam, will appear, and under Him man redeemed will again have all things put under his feet. What has been in the past shall be in the future.

God executed his judgments in the past. He will do so again. The past has manifested His power and glory; so will the future. The heavens will not always be silent as they are now; for "Surely our God shall come, and not keep silence."

His blessed Son was once upon earth, making known the glory of God in His Person. That was in the past, and it shall be so again; for He comes back to the earth once more to make known His glory, so that the earth shall be covered with the glory of the Lord.

How near, how very near, these things that shall be are! The age in which we live is the last stepping stone towards the glorious consummation; and in this age there is but a little step left, and soon darkest night shall end and give way to the brightest and most glorious day the world has ever seen. In these studies of Prophecy we shall first consider the present age, its beginning, progress and end. Other studies will put before us from the infallible Word of God the coming glorious consummation and what leads up to it.

I

The Beginning of the Age. In dealing with man and the earth, to work out his own plan of redemption and restoration, God works in certain periods of time which are called ages. Each age has a definite beginning and a definite end. All the different ages which preceded our own age were ages of preparation, for the present age in which we live. In every past age God announced the coming of Him by whom He not only created all things, but by whom He made the ages, that is, His Son. He is the One in whom and for whom all is planned, and through whom the things which have been shall be again, and infinitely more.

He was first announced in the Garden of Eden as the Seed of the woman who should bruise the serpent's head. In the age after the flood Shem was singled out in whom the Name, that is, the Lord of Glory, should be revealed. Then Abraham, a son of Shem received the promise in the Patriarchal Age that He would come from his seed; and later in the Jewish Age He was promised as the Son of David, and David knew Him by the Spirit as his Lord.

And so in the fulness of time He came, born of a woman, made under the Law, the Son of God manifested in the flesh. His blessed earth life belongs still to the Jewish dispensation, the age which preceded our own age. He came as the minister of the circumcision; and as such He fulfilled the Law and moved exclusively among His own people Israel, bringing them the message of the Kingdom promised to that nation; a Kingdom in which righteousness and peace is to flourish, and into which all the nations of the earth are to be gathered.

The Jewish prophets had announced that Kingdom, but through God's foreknowledge it was also made known that Christ should suffer first, and be rejected by His people; and this came to pass. The nation instead of giving Him the throne to which He is entitled, delivered their own King into the hands of the Gentiles to be crucified. What Gabriel in his great message had communicated to Daniel, that Messiah should be cut off and receive nothing, happened, and that in the very time as revealed in the ninth chapter of Daniel. The Son of God died, rejected by His own nation, He died the sinner's death, He died for the ungodly, He died so that the flood-gates of Divine love and grace might be opened; and that a Holy God might be justified in saving believing sinners, both Jews and Gentiles, and making them the heirs of glory.

Our age then begins with this fact: Christ rejected by His own people, cast out by the world, finishing on the Cross the work of sin bearing. With this, and the associated events, our age started in. Let us see then what we find in the beginning of this age, and then see how the things we shall mention are affected as this age progresses and comes finally to its close.

First, as to the Lord Jesus Christ. As we have already stated, the Son of God came to this earth, was rejected by men, put to death on the cross, and after His burial God raised Him from the dead and gave Him glory. In due time He left the earth and ascended in His glorified human body into heaven, where He is seated now at the right hand of the majesty on high. It is a wonderful fact that in heaven, seated at God's own right hand, there is a Man. One who was born of the Virgin, lived on earth a holy life, died the sinner's death on the Cross, was buried and raised by the power of God. Before this age He was also in heaven, but not as man. He was ever in the bosom of the Father as the Only Begotten. Now as the Man Christ Jesus who has conquered He fills that throne, the Father's throne. He has not His own throne which belongs to Him, nor will He get this throne, the throne of His father David, as long as this age lasts. Exalted in the highest place He has all power, and exercises in behalf of His people, His priesthood and His advocacy, ministering to the needs of His own on earth.

Second, let us see next about the Holy Spirit in His relation to this age. He came to earth on the day of Pentecost. In the Old Testament times He visited the earth, but not to abide, as is now the case. He strove with men from the very beginning, He endued prophets, and priests and kings, and all who believed the Word of God, of which He is the Author; but after Christ died and had gone back to the Father, He came as the other Comforter, the One who takes the place of the absent Christ. He is come to earth to accomplish God's purpose in this present age. Nowhere do we read in the New Testament that the purpose of the coming of the Holy Spirit is to convert the world, and establish universal righteousness and peace. These blessings are not promised for the age in which we live. The great purpose for which the Spirit of God came in the beginning of our age is for the out-taking of the Church, the Body of Christ. He is gathering together Jews and Gentiles who believe on Christ and puts them into this Body. On the Day of Pentecost this Body began; then all the gathered believers were baptised by the One Spirit into one Body. This work continues throughout this age. Then He Himself bestows the gifts which are needed for the upbuilding of that Body. In the beginning of this age He unfolded His special energy in sign gifts, confirming by these the truth of Christianity. These special gifts and signs were only confined to the beginning of the age. Nowhere is it stated that they were to continue to the end, for this age is an age of faith and not of sight.

Third, during this age there is preached a special message which was unknown in former ages. This message is the Gospel of Grace. It is true that before Christ died an innumerable company of people were saved, and salvation of course was always by grace. They believed God, confessed themselves sinners, trusted in the promise, and then they were saved. But the Gospel message as it began to be preached after Christ died and the Holy Spirit came to earth, was not known in Old Testament times. That Gospel not only offers remission of sins, but tells the believing sinner that he becomes in Christ a Son of God and a joint heir with the Lord Jesus Christ; that eternal life is his present possession and

6

that he is one spirit with the Lord, for the Holy Spirit makes His abode in him. This then is the great message which was preached with the beginning of this age, and which is to be preached to its very end. It is the only power of God unto salvation, and anything else is a miserable, good-for-nothing substitute and counterfeit, which not alone cannot please God, but upon which the curse of God rests; for anything short of the Gospel of Christ is an insult to God and a denial of His righteousness and love. And this Gospel is to be preached according to the word of our Lord beginning in Jerusalem, in Judea, and Samaria, and to the uttermost ends of the earth. This Divine program given by our Lord has been carried out; the preaching began in Jerusalem, that is where the Gospel stream started; from there it flowed into Judea and Samaria, and then Gentiles heard the Gospel and were saved. Our Lord indicated this world-wide sowing during this age in the first parable of Matthew xiii, when He spoke of the sower going out into the field, telling us that the field is the world. Israel in the preceding age was spoken of as a vineyard with a fence about, but in this age there is no more vineyard, no more special place where labor is to be done; but as John Wesley used to say, "The world is my parish."

Fourth, let us also notice that with the beginning of the age there is made known the full Truth of God by revelation. It is the faith which is once and for all delivered unto the saints. When our Lord was on earth He spoke repeatedly to His disciples that He had many things to say unto them, which they could not grasp, but that they should know them afterward. The "afterward" does not mean heaven, but it means the afterward of the Holy Spirit. He told them that when the Spirit came He would take of these things of Christ and show them unto them; and so when He came He brought with Him the fullest revelation concerning Christ Himself, the believer's position in Him and all the gracious truths connected with it. In this sense, the Word of God was completed in the beginning of this age. Nothing can be added to it, nor must anything be taken away from it. There is no such thing as progress in the Truth of God, that man by research can discover something for himself, as he attempts to do in the different sciences. The Truth and doctrine made known in the beginning of this age is a fixed Truth, it is eternal Truth, it is unchangeable Truth, and as such the only light which man has during this age.

Fifth, as to the moral characteristics of this age. The Apostle John tells us that the world lieth in the wicked one, and that the character of the world is antagonistic to the Word of God. The age therefore is branded in every portion of the New Testament as an evil age. Certain exhortations to believers make this clear. All exhortations in the New Testament to

Christians are exhortations to separate from this age. In the beginning of Galatians we are expressly told that the Lord Jesus Christ gave Himself for our sins that He might deliver us out of this present evil age. Then again we read what Paul wrote to Titus that the grace of God has appeared bringing salvation to all men, teaching us that we should deny ungodliness and worldly lusts, and should live soberly, righteously and godly in this present age. This shows that the present age is evil.

And nowhere is the promise made in the Epistles that this present age can ever be anything different than an evil age. It continues evil to the end.

Sixth, what is the relation of Satan to our age? He is the enemy of God, and seemingly achieved a triumph when he got man to reject the Lord of Glory. On this account He is called in the New Testament "the god of this age." He is the domineering spirit of the age in which we live, which is also called Man's Day. Christ is rejected, with no throne on earth, but Satan instead has his throne in this world and controls the affairs of the age. That this is so may be seen from the very events with which this age started. Persecution soon set in, believers were slain, and in every other way this dark shadow antagonized the work of the Spirit and counterfeited the Truth of God. Therefore the spiritual warfare of believers in this age is to stand against the wiles of the devil, for we wrestle not against flesh and blood, but against principalities, against the powers, against the world rulers of this darkness, against the wicked spirits in the heavenly places. (Eph. vi:12). From this we learn that the age is ruled over by Satan and the wicked spirits.

Seventh, there is another item which needs to be mentioned in connection with the beginning of this age, and that is the Jewish people. Their measure of wickedness was filled when they delivered the Son of God into the hands of the Gentiles to be crucified. God in mercy lingered over the city for forty years before the announced judgment was executed upon the city and upon the nation. Thousands upon thousands repented and accepted the Gospel; in fact, the beginning of the entire Church was Jewish. But the nation hardened its heart, and finally the tears which the Lord had shed over Jerusalem were justified in the awful siege of Jerusalem, followed by the dispersion of the nation. Ever since they have been in fulfillment of the predictions of their own prophets, scattered amongst the nations of the world, and this is continuing throughout this age.

We see then that there is a marked difference between this age and the ages which preceded it. Christ as the glorified Man in heaven, the Holy Spirit on earth, a new message, a new work which the Spirit of God does, the full revelation of God given to men, the world in darkness, Satan its god, and the Jews no longer in their land but wandering amongst the nations with judicial blindness upon them.

II

The Progress of the Age. This present age is unrevealed in the Old Testament. When Daniel received the great prophecy which Gabriel carried from the Throne of God to the praying Prophet, he heard that at a certain time the death of Christ should take place, and that the city and the sanctuary should be burned, and the nation scattered. This was at the close of the sixty-ninth week, four hundred and eighty-three years after the command to rebuild the wall of Jerusalem had been given. As we have shown in our book on Daniel this has been literally fulfilled, and as all students of prophecy know there is an unfulfilled week, or seven years, which are yet to come to pass in the history of that nation. The space between the sixty-ninth and the seventieth week is this present age. Nor is there anywhere in the Word of God a revelation which tells us of the duration of this age. There is no hint about it in the Old Testament; and when the disciples asked the Lord about the restoration of the Kingdom to Israel, which manifestly takes place at the close of this age, He told them, "It is not for you to know the times and the seasons." It is therefore useless trying to find out about the duration of the age.

But when we come to the moral and religious characteristics, in connection with the progress of this age, it is different. They are fully revealed by the Lord and also by His Spirit. Especially is this true of the very end of this age. Twice our Lord spoke on these matters, once on earth when He gave the Kingdom parables in Matthew xiii and spoke of the progress of the age and what should take place during His absence. Again He spoke from heaven about these same things, when He gave the messages to the seven churches. In them He outlined the course of the professing church on earth, and reveals in it what is to take place during the progress of this age.

We shall cover the same seven things which we have mentioned in connection with the beginning of this age, and learn how they are affected as this age progresses and nears its end.

First, as to the Lord Jesus Christ in glory. Enthroned in the highest glory He can never be affected by what is going on down here. Satan's power cannot reach Him. The Lord Jesus is the same, yesterday, today, and forever. Whatever man does on earth, however great the hatred may be against Him, even if the nations unite to cast off His cords and bands, in the language of the second Psalm, "He that sitteth in the heavens shall laugh at them and hold them in derision." But there is a comforting truth in connection with this, the comfort of which has been the blessed portion of all God's people as the age progressed, and its true character became more and more known. "Saul, Saul, why persecutest thou me," was the word the Lord Jesus addressed to the persecutor of the Church of God. It shows His loving interest and sympathy for His suffering members on earth. And so as the age progressed in the pagan persecutions and the equally bad, if not worse, Papal persecutions, He has sustained His people on earth, He has never failed them, He has carried them through the water and through the fire. He has presented their petitions before the Throne of God, and answered their prayers. Nor will He ever fail His people until they are gathered home into His presence, the trophies of His grace.

Second. Nor can the Holy Spirit and His work be affected by what the progress of this age brings. He knows no failure. His Divine mission cannot fail. In every generation during this age, no matter how dark it may have been, He has continued successfully His work and added to the Body of Christ, in each generation those who believed on the Son of God.

Third and Fourth, as to the Gospel and the Truth of God it is different, for we shall notice here at once what the progress of the age has brought about in connection with what God has given to this age. Our Lord tells us in the second parable, in Matthew xiii, that no sooner had the wheat, the Truth, been sown in the field, which is the world, but that an enemy came and sowed the tares. Then He revealed this fact that the wheat and the tares were to grow together until the harvest, which is the end of the age. There is then a development in the progress of this age, a development in the wheat, which is ripening for the harvest, and the development of the tares. The Truth is to shine more brightly as the age progresses, and darkness becomes more dense. We see therefore that after a brief period of purity the evil began in the professing church. The Gospel, even in Apostolic days was being denied, and the Apostles' doctrines corrupted.

What the Lord Jesus taught in the parable of the mustard seed came also to pass as the age progressed. The little mustard seed became a great tree, and the birds began to lodge in its branches to defile the tree. The professing church became a great world institution, and in alliance with the world where the throne of Satan is, became corrupted; instead of being the espoused virgin, she became the harlot and adultress. What the Lord Jesus announced in the Parable of the leaven came likewise to pass as this age progressed. The leaven, which is corruption, evil in every form, especially in Christian doctrine, has been introduced into the pure doctrine of Christ, the three measures of fine wheat.

10

And so we see that as the age progressed the rejection of every phase of Divine Truth set in. The Deity of Christ denied, the Virgin Birth, His atoning death, His physical resurrection, everything denied; the Bible as the revelation of God rejected; and with these denials there came the increase of unrighteousness and moral declension, till the age produced the condition which the Word of God clearly foresaw, a great professing church, with the harlot character, unfaithful to Christ and to His Word; while of course it is equally true that there is the true Church, which remains true to Christ and to His Word.

Fifth, as the age progresses there is no change seen in the condition of the world. It is true man has been developing Man's Day. As the age progressed great inventions and discoveries were made. These are often taken to be indications that the age is getting better. They point to the telephone, and wireless, the great engineering feats, the chemical discoveries, and everything else in these lines as evidences that the age is constantly improving. Before the war we were told that the age had improved to such an extent that a great war would no longer be possible. Everybody was lauding our great civilization to the skies. A few weeks after everything was knocked sky-high, and what is left of all these optimistic ramblings? No, this age does not improve, and everything which the Word of God has to say about it has been solemnly verified and confirmed by the roar of cannons and by the slaughter of millions. Our great inventions and discoveries have not made the world more righteous. On the contrary, unrighteousness and lawlessness have increased, and later we shall show how everything in these conditions points to the very end of this age.

Sixth, Satan. The world does not change, neither does Satan. He can never be anything else but the enemy of God, nor can his person and work be arrested by man's efforts. As the age continues his opposition becomes more marked. We know from the lips of our Lord that he is the liar and the murderer from the beginning. He has made good these titles throughout this age. He tried to stamp out more than once the Truth of Christ by instigating the cruel persecutions of the people of God. They were slain by the thousands and hundreds of thousands during the reign of the Roman Emperors. When he failed in this then he manifested his character as the liar from the beginning. He began to counterfeit the Truth, and partially succeeded in corrupting the professing church and putting a spurious system in control, where he makes good his title as the liar. When in the progress of this age the Spirit of God began reviving the Truth, when the noble men and women refused to bow before Rome, he again acted as the murderer. Thousands upon thousands were tortured, slain, and burned alive, until he discovered that the Truth cannot be

11

stamped out by the fires of persecution, that he was failing again as he had failed in the first century of the age. Then once more he appears in the garb of an angel of light. Now he does his work through demon-cults like Christian Science, Spiritism, Mormonism and others. He manifests himself once more as the liar from the beginning in the New Theology and the Destructive Criticism, so widely accepted everywhere. And thus he continues his work as the age progresses; no change for the better.

Seventh, as already stated the Jews are wanderers amongst the nations. We know two things concerning the Jews. The first is that they are given the promise in earthly things, and though they are now blinded, God has not cast them away; and the other is that they are during this age under judgment. These two facts stand out in the history of that remarkable people as the age continues. If we want to see the richest people, the most influential, the brightest, we must turn to the Jewish people. In that fact God witnesses that they are still His people. And then the greatest sorrow, the greatest suffering, the greatest poverty is found amongst them; the witness that they are under judgment. Over and over again in every century has solemnly come to pass what their forefathers cried, "His blood be upon us, and upon our children." We shall later point out the startling change which is coming upon them as a nation when the age ends.

III

The End of the Age. Like every previous age, our age will also come to a close. It is here we find one of the vital errors amongst Christians at the present time. They never think of this age of Gospel preaching and Gospel privilege as coming to an end. If one speaks to them about the end of the age, they think it means after the world is converted, and the passing away of the world itself. Peter has given us the witness that this would be one of the characteristics of the last days, when mockers shall come, saying, "Where is the promise of His coming? for from the day the fathers fell asleep all things continue as they were from the beginning of the creation." This is what we find so much in our day. In spite of the horrible conditions in which this age has been plunged, and the confirmation of the predictions of the Bible relating to this age, the mass of professing Christians expect that things will continue, and that after the war the age will speedily improve. We have seen before how impossible this is, for the Bible teaches us that this age is an evil age, and there is not a single passage which promises an improvement. On the contrary, everything in the Word shows that as the age ends, and its real end comes, all the evil conditions present in this age come to a head and climax. We find therefore a great deal said in the Scriptures about the end of the age. The Lord Jesus speaks of it in His parables in Matthew xiii. He has given also a complete panorama of the age-ending in His great Olivet discourse. Then when we come to the Epistles we find that the Spirit of God through every writer gives a warning and a witness about the end of the age. All these warnings and witnesses do not tell us of a converted world, and a world which is won to righteousness, of nations who lay down their armaments and no longer make war; nor do these warnings and predictions speak of a triumph of the doctrine of Christ. They tell us the very opposite. They give warnings that the faith is going to be rejected, that delusions and errors are going to multiply, that nation is going to lift up sword against nation and kingdom against kingdom, that lawlessness and unrighteousness are going to increase, and that the age itself is going to end in a time of trouble such as the world has never seen before.

If we turn to the last Book of the Bible we find also an argument concerning the age and its end. Before the heaven opens and He comes, whose right it is to establish His Kingdom over this earth, the wicked and wild conditions prevailing on this earth are described, and that on account of them the judgments of the Lord will be in the earth.

And now to follow the same line of thought as in our preceding meditations, let us again notice the same things which we mentioned before in connection with the beginning and progress of this age.

First, as this age comes to a close Christ is still on the Father's Throne. His ministry in behalf of His people both as Priest and Advocate continues unbroken. He has promised, "Lo, I am with you always even unto the end of the age." We say again, He changes not. As He sustained His people in the beginning of the age and gave them victory, as He kept the feet of His saints in every generation and gathered them home into His own presence, so He will still minister to the needs of His members on earth. Let the age become as dark as it possibly can, His people who trust in Him and walk in His fellowship will be kept and preserved. We do not know all that is going on in glory. We know he is there as the upholder of all things. We know that the greater part of the children of God are as disembodied spirits in His presence. Some day a startling thing will happen in that glory. The hour has come when the redeemed are to have their resurrection bodies, and all the living saints shall be changed in a moment, in the twinkling of an eye. When that hour strikes He Himself will arise from the place at the Father's right hand and pass out of the third heaven, and then from the air give the shout which will summon all the redeemed to meet Him in the sky. For this the people of God are waiting in the end of this age.

[1] See article "That Blessed Hope." [Transcriber's note: there was no matching footnote number in the above text, so it is not known what this footnote referred to.]

Second, the Holy Spirit also remains the same. His energy is undiminished. The work He came to do and which He has done throughout this age, will be done by Him to the very end. Indeed, while darkness increases and the enemy becomes more active, God's people may confidently expect that the Holy Spirit will also demonstrate His power in the behalf of those who love and walk in the Truth. Some day He will have finished the work for which He came, the Body will be complete as to numbers; and when that crowning event, the coming of the Lord for His saints, takes place, the Holy Spirit will have His part to do. Not alone Christ will present the Church but the Holy Spirit as well; and then He will leave the earth, no longer to be here to do the special work which He came to do on the Day of Pentecost. He has finished the work.

Third, the Gospel is still preached during the end of the age. As long as the Church remains here the true Gospel testimony can never be silenced, because behind it stands the omnipotent Spirit of God and the power of Christ. But as the age closes the true Gospel is being more and more rejected. We see this today; we hear on all hands that man no longer needs to be born again, that the blood of Christ cannot save, that character saves; that the soldiers who die on the battlefield bring a sacrifice like Christ brought on the Cross, and that the hero's death makes all things right in the past life and opens the gates of glory. On all sides we see these rejections; the Son of God is denied and every phase of His work is set aside. This is exactly what is taught in the New Testament, that men would turn away their ears from the Truth, and that the great mass of professing Christians would only have a form of godliness and deny the power thereof.

When at last the Church has ended her ministry the sound of the Gospel of Grace will no longer be heard. While this is true, on the other hand the Gospel still preached up to the end of the age brings about the completion of the Body of Christ. We see this today in a startling manner. While amongst the so-called Christian nations the Gospel is rejected, in heathen countries the Gospel is accepted by thousands upon thousands, and thus the Body of Christ, the true Church, is being made complete.

Fourth, when this age closes the whole body of the doctrine of Christ and the Truth will be rejected. The foundation for this has gradually been laid. It started over a hundred years ago in Germany, where the modern criticism of the Bible started. This criticism has constantly been growing, until everywhere throughout Christendom an infallible Bible is being denied. Thus the foundations of the faith have been undermined, and the way is prepared for the final apostasy, the complete falling away from the Truth.

Fifth, in regard to the world. As stated previously this age cannot get better, but becomes worse. We see it today, how all inventions and discoveries in which we used to boast as evidences of progress are being made use of in the most horrible catastrophe the world has ever seen. Europe is like a human slaughterhouse. Nations are against nations and kingdoms against kingdoms; and all this was started by a nation which boasted of having the most light in religious things and the best culture and civilization. And all along they denied Christ and the Truth of God; and when the outbreak came it was only a demonstration that behind their Christless civilization and culture there stood the domineering shadow of the prince of this world. When we look closer into the Prophetic Word we find that these conditions continue to the end of the age, and that finally there comes a tremendous crash, when the Lord Himself will deal with these horrible conditions and smite the wicked and the ungodly.

But some one might say, "What is the use of doing anything at all if this is the program?" "What is the use of us to fight as a nation?" But this is wrong logic. There are principles of righteousness and justice which must be maintained in this world, for which man must stand up, and as far as our nation is concerned we are on the side of justice and the defense of righteousness, which have the approval of God, for they are in line with His righteous government. When the time comes for the reckoning, not from the human side but from God's side, this will fall heavily into the scale when the nations are judged.

Sixth, as to Satan. Like a huge serpent he has been winding his way throughout this age, leaving everywhere his contamination. While Satan is not omniscient and perfect in knowledge, he has sufficient knowledge of his destiny and how soon that destiny will be accomplished, and so as the age closes he becomes fiercer in his wrath; like a serpent which is attacked and in danger of being caught, his hiss is heard on all sides. He is now actively engaged in counterfeiting the Truth, in putting in his demon doctrines, in perverting the Truth wherever he can. And by and by after the true Church is gone he will put his masterpieces into the world, of whom we shall have more to say in these studies. Then he will blind

15

the nations as never before and rush them on to the final climax of the age.

Seventh, as to the Jews. We have seen how they were scattered at the beginning of this age, and how they continued to wander amongst the nations as the age progressed. When we come to the end of the age a startling change takes place with His people. The figtree, once cursed, puts forth new leaves; the dry bones of the house of Israel begin to show signs of life. There is a movement amongst them, bone comes to bone, they organize, their faces are turned towards the east; they are getting ready for the greatest event in all history. The Lord Jesus Christ said that Jerusalem should be trodden down of the Gentiles until the times of the Gentiles are fulfilled. When the end of the age comes the times of the Gentiles are about fulfilled; and the startling sign that the age ends is the movement amongst the Jews so prominent today. The capture of Jerusalem and the complete downfall of the Turk are significant signs. Palestine will be given to the Jews when the war ends. Then the stage is set, so to speak, for the predicted end of the age.

We have rapidly pointed out the leading features of the beginning, progress and end of this age. The real end is composed of seven years, the last prophetic week of Daniel's prophecy (Dan. ix). The true church will then no longer be on the earth. Her translation has taken place. The Saints are with the Lord. But on earth the things will come to pass which are so prominently revealed in the prophetic Word. And when the seven years are over the Lord Jesus Christ will come back in power and glory to establish His Kingdom of righteousness and peace. Then that which has been shall be again and still greater glory added.

"THAT BLESSED HOPE"

"Looking for that blessed hope, and the glorious appearing of the glory of our great God and our Saviour Jesus Christ," Tit. ii:13.

"That blessed hope" of which the Apostle writes is an exclusively New Testament revelation. The appearing of the glory of our great God and our Savior Jesus Christ is fully revealed in the Old Testament prophetic Word. The Prophets had visions of the day of the Lord, a day in which the Lord will be manifested in power and glory; a day which will bring glory and peace when the Lord is enthroned as King of kings and Lord of lords. The Spirit of God has shown through the prophets what the appearing, the visible manifestation of the Lord will mean, for the people Israel, for the nations and for groaning creation. But nowhere do we find "that blessed hope" made known by the prophets. The Jewish Saints knew nothing of it as it is revealed to the church of God. True they had now and then a glimpse of the future. One of the greatest sufferers was Job. His darkest night was illuminated by the assurance of hope when he uttered his great testimony: "I know that my Redeemer liveth, and that He shall stand in the latter day upon the earth. And if after my skin this body shall be destroyed, yet in my flesh shall I see God. Whom I shall see for myself, and mine eyes shall behold, and not another" (Job xix:25-27). But this is not "that blessed hope" the Lord has given to us His people.

Old Testament Saints knew of the resurrection of the dead. They knew nothing of a resurrection from among the dead. Yet Enoch and Elijah were taken to glory without dying. No prophet knew the typical meaning of their experience as we know it through "that blessed hope."

For the First Time

"That blessed hope" is for the first time mentioned by our Lord. But where in His earthly life did He give it to His disciples? It is not found in the records of the three first Gospels, generally called the synoptics. In these records He spoke often of His Return. He promised a Second Coming of Himself in the clouds of heaven with power and great glory. He revealed what should take place before His return. In His prophetic Olivet discourse (Matt. xxiv-xxv) He gave the signs of His Coming, the preceding great tribulation, the physical signs accompanying His visible manifestation, the regathering of His elect people Israel by the angels. He revealed how some would then be taken in judgment and others left on the earth to enter the Kingdom (Matt. xxiv:40-41). He also spoke in parables of how the conditions in Christendom would be dealt with by Him. And finally He gave a prophecy concerning the judgment of the living nations in the day of His appearing. But nowhere in the Gospels of Matthew, Mark and Luke did He speak of "that blessed hope."

It was in the upper room discourse that He spoke of it the first time. His eleven disciples were gathered about Him. Judas had gone out into the night to betray Him. For him of whom the Lord said it would have been better had he never been born, there was no blessed hope. The Lord had announced His imminent departure from them. He would leave them. When Peter said "I will lay down my life for thy sake" (John xiii:30), the omniscient One told him, "the cock shall not crow till thou hast denied me thrice." How sorrowful this little company must have been! Despair was probably on all their faces. Their hearts were greatly troubled.

17

Then His beloved voice broke the silence and uttered the never to be forgotten words, "Let not your heart be troubled; ye believe in God, believe also in Me. In my Father's house are many mansions; if it were not so I would have told you. I go to prepare a place for you; and if I go and prepare a place for you, I will come again, and receive you unto Myself that where I am ye may be also" (John xiv:1-3). In these words "that blessed hope" is mentioned for the first time in the Bible.

What It Is

Only those who belonged to Him heard this promise. It is therefore a promise not given to Israel, or to the world, but only for those who know Him as their Savior and Lord, who have believed on Him and are His own. The promise is twofold. He would come again and receive them unto Himself; and that He would take them to the place where He is. And this is "that blessed hope." His coming for His own to be with Him in the Father's house to occupy the mansions He has prepared by His atoning work.

The contrast of this promise of His Coming for His disciples with the promises of His visible return as given in the synoptics is striking. He does not say a word about any signs. He does not mention the great tribulation. Nor has He anything to say about judgment. He only gives the assurance that He, in person, will come again and then receive them unto Himself. They were not to look for certain signs and events as predicted in Daniel's prophecy, or wait for the great tribulation and the manifestation of the man of sin. His promise told them to wait for Himself.

His Prayer

A little while later after He had given this promise of His Coming for them they heard Him pray. This prayer is found in the seventeenth chapter of John. What a prayer it is! As they listened to His voice addressing the Father they had new glimpses of His great love wherewith He loved them. He prayed for their sanctification, for their preservation and finally for their glorification. He made a demand of the Father which confirmed the promise He had previously given to them. He prayed, "Father, I will that they, whom Thou hast given Me be with Me where I am, that they may behold my glory which thou hast given Me, for Thou lovedst Me before the foundation of the world" (John xvii:24). In these words He asks the Father to do what He had promised His disciples. His own are to be with Him where He is, to behold His glory.

18

An Unfulfilled Promise and an Unanswered Prayer

The promise of "that blessed hope" given so long ago is still unfulfilled; the prayer He prayed is not yet answered. Some say that when our Lord said "I will come again and receive you unto myself" He meant the death of the believer. This is positively wrong. When the believer dies the Lord does not come to the individual believer, but the believer goes to be with the Lord. "Absent from the body present with the Lord." When the believer dies his body is put into the ground, while the disembodied part goes straight into His presence. But the body is also redeemed and must be fashioned like unto His glorious body. The disciples died and generations upon generations of believers passed away and the promise is still unfulfilled and His prayer not yet answered.

The Full Revelation

The disciples, though they knew the promise of "that blessed hope" had no knowledge whatever how the Lord would come again and receive them unto Himself. He did not reveal the manner of His Coming when He spoke to them. The Lord singled out the Apostle Paul to give to him the special revelation as to the manner of His Coming for His Saints and how "that blessed hope" would some day be fulfilled. The Apostle Paul is the instrument through whom the Lord was pleased to give the highest revelation in the Word of God, so that he could say that it was given to him "to fulfil (complete) the Word of God." To him the full glory of the church, the body of Christ, was made known, and through this chosen vessel, who called himself less than the least of all the Saints, the full revelation of "that blessed hope" is given.

The first Epistle he wrote was the Epistle to the Thessalonians. The great revelation of the blessed hope is found in the first Epistle. "But we do not wish you to be ignorant concerning them that are fallen asleep, to the end that ye sorrow not, even as others who have no hope. For if we believe that Jesus died and rose again, so also God will bring with Him those who have fallen asleep through Jesus. For this we say to you in the Word of the Lord, that we, the living, who remain to the coming of the Lord, are in no way to anticipate those who have fallen asleep: for the Lord Himself will descend from heaven with an assembling shout, with the voice of the archangel and with the trump of God; and the dead in Christ shall rise first; then we, the living who remain, shall be caught up together with them in clouds, to meet the Lord in the air; and so shall we ever be with the Lord. Wherefore comfort one another with these words" (1 Thess. iv:13-18,—corrected translation). These words, so unique and precious, give the full revelation about "the blessed hope." Some of the

Thessalonian believers had died and those who were left behind feared that their departed ones had lost their share in the coming glorious meeting with the Lord. On their account they sorrowed like those who have no hope. And so the Lord gave to the Apostle this special revelation to quiet their fears and to enlighten them as to the details of the coming of the Lord for all His Saints, those who had fallen asleep, and those who live when He fulfills His promise. The little church of Thessalonica with these sorrowing Saints was made the recipient of this great and comforting message which is for the whole body of Christ as well.

Let us examine it. "For if we believe that Jesus died and rose again, so also God will bring with Him those who have fallen asleep through Jesus." Here is first the blessed fact that "Jesus died." Of the Saints it is said that they fell asleep; but never is it said that Jesus slept, when He gave His life on the cross. He tasted death, the death in all its unfathomable meaning as the judgment upon sin. For the saints the physical death is but sleep.[1] And He who died rose again; as certainly as He died and rose again, so surely shall all believers rise. God will bring all those who have fallen asleep through Jesus with Him, that is with the Lord when He comes in the day of His glorious manifestation. It does not mean the receiving of them by the Lord, nor does it mean that He brings their disembodied spirits with Him to be united to their bodies from the graves, but it means that those who have fallen asleep will God bring with His Son when He comes with all His saints; they will all be in that glorified company. When the Lord comes back from glory all the departed saints will be with Him. This is what the Thessalonians needed to know first of all. Before we follow this blessed revelation in its unfolding we call attention to the phrase "fallen asleep through (not in) Jesus;" it may also be rendered by "those who were put to sleep by Jesus." His saints in life and death are in His hands. When saints put their bodies aside, it is because their Lord has willed it so. "Precious in the sight of the Lord is the death of His saints" (Ps. cxvi:15). When our loved ones leave us, may we think of their departure as being "put to sleep by Jesus."

But blessed as this answer to their question is, it produced another difficulty. Hearing that the saints who had fallen asleep would come with the Lord on the day of His glorious manifestation, they would ask, "How is it possible that they can come with Him?" Are they coming as disembodied spirits? What about their bodies in the graves? How shall they come with Him? To answer these questions the special revelation "by the Word of the Lord" is given, by which they learned, and we also, how they would all be with Him so as to come with Him at His appearing. "For this we say to you by the Word of the Lord, that we, the living, who remain unto the coming of the Lord, are in no wise to anticipate those who have fallen asleep." He tells them that when the Lord comes for His saints, those who have fallen asleep will not have an inferior place, and that, we, the living, who remain to the coming of the Lord, will not precede those who have fallen asleep. When Paul wrote these words and said "We, the living, who remain," he certainly considered himself as included in that class. The two companies who will meet the Lord when He comes, those who have fallen asleep and those who are living, are mentioned here for the first time. How the living saints will not precede those who have departed and the order in which the coming of the Lord for His saints will be executed is next made known in this wonderful revelation.

"For the Lord Himself will descend from heaven with an assembling shout, with the voice of the archangel and with the trump of God; and the dead in Christ shall rise first, then, we, the living, who remain, shall be caught up together with them in clouds, to meet the Lord in the air, and so shall we ever be with the Lord. Wherefore comfort one another with these words." This is the full revelation of the blessed hope in its manner of fulfilment. Nothing like it is found anywhere in the Old Testament Scriptures. In writing later to the Corinthians Paul mentioned it again: "Behold I show you a mystery; we shall not all sleep, but we shall all be changed. In a moment, in the twinkling of an eye, at the last trump; for the trumpet shall sound, and the dead shall be raised incorruptible, and we shall be changed" (1 Cor. xv:51-52).

The Lord *Himself* will descend from heaven. He is now at the right hand of God in glory, crowned with honor and glory. There He exercises His Priesthood and advocacy in behalf of His people, by which He keeps, sustains and restores them. When the last member has been added to the church, which is His body, and that body is to be with Him, who is the head, He will leave the place at the right hand and descend from heaven. He will not descend to the earth, for, as we read later, the meeting-place for Him and His saints is the air and not the earth. When He comes with His saints in His visible manifestation, He will descend to the earth. When He comes for His Saints He comes with a shout. It denotes His supreme authority. The Greek word is "Kelusma," which means literally "a shout of command," used in classical Greek for the hero's shout to his followers in battle, the commanding voice to gather together. He ascended with a shout (Ps. lxvii:5), and with the victor's shout He returns. The shout may be the single word "Come!" "Come and see" He spoke to the disciples who followed Him and inquired for His dwelling place. Before Lazarus' tomb He spoke with a loud voice, "Come forth." John, in the isle of Patmos, after the throne messages to the churches had

21

been given, saw a door opened in heaven and the voice said "Come up hither" (Rev. iv:1). "Come" is the royal word of grace, and grace will do its supreme work when He comes for His own. But there will also be the voice of the archangel (Michael) and the trump of God. The archangel is the leader of the angelic hosts. As He was seen of angels (1 Tim. iii:16) when He ascended into the highest heaven, so will the archangel be connected with His descent out of heaven. All heaven will be in commotion when the heirs of glory, sinners saved by grace, are about to be brought with glorified bodies into the Father's house. Some teach that the voice of the archangel may be employed to summon the heavenly hosts and marshal the innumerable company of the redeemed, for "They shall gather His elect together from the four winds, from one end of heaven to the other" (Matthew xxiv:30-31). But this is incorrect. The elect in Matthew xxiv are not the church, but Israel. Dispersed Israel will be regathered and angels will be used in this work. Furthermore the angels will do this gathering after the great tribulation and after the visible manifestation of the Lord with His saints. The coming of the Lord for His saints takes place before the great tribulation.

The trump of God is also mentioned. This trumpet has nothing to do with the judgment trumpets of Revelation, nor with the Jewish feast of trumpets. Some teach that the trumpet is the last trumpet of Revelation. But note the trumpet here is the trumpet of God; in Revelation the last trumpet is blown by an angel. It is a symbolical term and like the shout stands for the gathering together. In Numbers x:4 we read, "And if they blow with one trumpet, then the princes, the heads of the thousands of Israel, shall gather themselves unto thee." The shout and the trump of God will gather the fellow-heirs of Christ. "The dead in Christ shall rise first." This is the resurrection from among all the dead of those who believed on Christ, the righteous, dead. All saints of all ages, Old and New Testament saints, are included. This statement of the resurrection of the dead in Christ first disposes completely of the unscriptural view of a general resurrection. As we know from Rev. xx:5 the rest of the dead (the wicked dead) will be raised up later. He comes in person to open the graves of all who belong to Him and manifests His authority over death which He has conquered. The dead in Christ will hear the shout first and experience His quickening power; they shall be raised incorruptible. What power will then be manifested! "Then we, the living, who remain, shall be caught up together with them in clouds to meet the Lord in the air; and so shall we ever be with the Lord." All believers who live on earth when the Lord comes will hear that commanding, gathering shout. It does not include those who only profess to be Christians and are nominal church-members, nor are any excluded who really are the

Lord's. The question, "Who will be caught up into glory?" is answered elsewhere in these studies. But see 1 Cor. xv:23 for an answer. The change will be "in a moment, in the twinkling of an eye" (1 Cor. xv:52). Then this mortal will put on immortality. It will be that "clothed upon" of which the apostle wrote to the Corinthians: "For in this tabernacle we groan, being burdened; not for that we would be unclothed (death) but clothed upon, that mortality might be swallowed up of life" (2 Cor. v:4). Then our body of humiliation will be fashioned like unto His own glorious body. It is the blessed, glorious hope, not death and the grave, but the coming of the Lord, when we shall be changed. And it is our imminent hope; believers must wait daily for it and some blessed day the shout will surely come.

When He descends from heaven with the shout and the dead in Christ are raised and we are changed, then "we shall be caught up together with them in clouds to meet the Lord in the air." It will be the blessed time of reunion with the loved ones who have gone before. What joy and comfort it must have brought to the sorrowing Thessalonians when they read these blessed words for the first time! And they are still the words of comfort and hope to all His people, when they stand at the open graves of loved ones who fell asleep as believers. Often the question is asked, "Shall we not alone meet our loved ones but also recognize them?" Here is the answer: "Together with them" implies both reunion and recognition. These words would indeed mean nothing did they not mean recognition. We shall surely see the faces of our loved ones again and all the saints of God on that blessed day when this great event takes place. The clouds will be heaven's chariots to take the heirs of God and the joint-heirs of the Lord Jesus Christ into His own presence. As He ascended so His redeemed ones will be taken up. Caught up in the clouds to meet the Lord in the air; all laws of gravitation are set aside, for it is the power of God, the same power which raised up the Lord Jesus from the dead and seated Him in glory, which will be displayed in behalf of His saints (Eph. i:19-23). Surely this is a divine and a wonderful revelation. "How foolish it must sound to our learned scientists. But, beloved, I would want nothing but that one sentence, 'Caught up in clouds to meet the Lord in the air,' to prove the divinity of Christianity. Its very boldness is assurance of its truth. No speculation, no argument, no reasoning; but a bare authoritative statement startling in its boldness. Not a syllable of Scripture on which to build, and yet when spoken, in perfect harmony with all Scripture. How absolutely impossible for any man to have conceived that the Lord's saints should be caught up to meet Him in the air. Were it not true its very boldness and apparent foolishness would be its refutation. And what would be the character of mind that could invent such a thought? What depths of wickedness! What cruelty! What callousness! The spring from which such a statement, if false, could rise must be corrupt indeed. But how different in fact! What severe righteousness! What depths of holiness! What elevated morality! What warmth of tender affection! What clear reasoning! Every word that he has written testifies that he has not attempted to deceive. Paul was no deceiver, and it is equally impossible for him to have been deceived."[2]

And the blessedness "to meet the Lord in the air"! We shall see Him then as He is and gaze for the first time upon the face of the Beloved, that face of glory, which was once marred and smitten on account of our sins. And seeing Him as He is we shall be like Him. How long will be the meeting in the air? It has been said that the stay in that meeting place will be but momentary and that the Lord will at once resume His descent to the earth. We know from other Scriptures that this cannot be. Between the coming of the Lord for His saints and with His saints there is an interval of at least seven years before the visible coming of the Lord and His saints with Him. The judgment of the saints, by which their works and labors become manifest must take place. There is also to be the presentation of the church in glory (Ephes. v:27; Jude verse 24). Furthermore the marriage of the Lamb takes place not in the meeting place in the air, but in heaven (Rev. xix:1-10). He will take His saints into the Father's house that they may behold His glory (John xvii:22). But what will it mean, "So shall we be forever with the Lord!"

Its Power and Blessedness

Such then is "that blessed hope," blessed indeed, and an imminent hope. It is a hope which if really held in the heart will shape the life and conduct of the believer, and fill, we make bold to say, every need he has in the wilderness down here.

1. That blessed hope will keep the person of the Lord Jesus Christ constantly before the heart. If we really look for Him, wait for Him, pray and long for His Coming, to see Him face to face, He will ever be fresh before our hearts. This hope will keep us in closest touch and fellowship with Him as nothing else. Oh! the blessedness of knowing we shall see Him—see Him in all His glory! Each day ought to be begun with this thought, "I may meet Him today!" Each day should have for its last thought the blessed anticipation that the coming morning may find us in His presence.

2. The blessed hope is a purifying hope. "He that has this hope set upon Him purifieth himself even as He is pure" (1 John iii:3). It is the power

for a consecrated and separated life. He prayed in His high-priestly prayer, "They are not of the world as I am not of the world. Sanctify them through Thy Truth, Thy Word is truth" (John xvii:16, 17). He has redeemed us from the curse, from the guilt of our sins and from this present evil age. We are saints, no longer of this world, though still in the world. With this comes the responsibility to live soberly, righteously and godly in this present age. If a child of God lives a worldly, carnal life it is a denial of the power of the Gospel. If a believer in that blessed hope lives an unholy life it is an evidence that he has never known in his heart what this hope is. It is a hope which teaches us to walk in the light as He is in the light. No believer who knows that blessed hope and waits for its fulfilment can go in the ways of the world to enjoy its hollow pleasures. It is a separating, purifying hope.

3. "That blessed hope" is furthermore a powerful incentive to service for God. One of the charges brought against this most precious doctrine is that it paralyses missionary work and all other activities. The very opposite is the case. It stimulates true service for God as nothing else does. Look at that great model servant, the Apostle Paul. What a witness he gives of his untiring, whole hearted service and the sufferings he endured in connection with it. Read 1 Thessalonians ii and 2 Corinthians xi:24-33. He had seen the Lord in glory and he knew that His glory belonged to him and that in the day of Christ he would see Him and receive the reward from His hands. This was the secret of his zeal for the Gospel; this gave him joy to endure. Like Moses he "had respect unto the recompense of the reward." He knew before the judgment seat of Christ he, and with him all the Saints, shall appear to receive the reward for faithful service. He looked upon those for whom he toiled, who were led to Christ by his testimony and nourished by his ministry as his glory and joy in the coming presence of the Lord. "For what is our hope, or joy, or crown of rejoicing? Are not even ye in the presence of our Lord Jesus Christ at His Coming? For ye are our glory and joy" (1 Thess. ii:19). The most successful evangelists and missionaries have been and are believers in that blessed hope. If we believe that He may come at any time, we shall certainly lose no time to do the work into which His grace has called us.

4. It is a sustaining hope. It sustains in suffering and in sorrow. David wrote: "The Lord will strengthen him upon the bed of languishing; thou wilt make all his bed in his sickness" (Ps. xli:3). It is the blessed hope of imminent glory which in sickness and pain gives strength, "yea songs in the night" will come from our lips if that blessed hope is ever first before our souls. And then it sustains the believer in conflict and keeps him faithful in the days of declension and apostasy.

25

5. It is a comforting hope. "Comfort one another with these words" the apostle wrote after he gave the great message. It is the comfort when our loved ones leave us. When we stand at the grave of the departed ones, who fell asleep in the Lord, we know that the day is coming when that grave opens and they come forth and we shall be united with them "caught up together with them to meet the Lord in the air."

[1] Some have perverted the meaning of "sleep," and instead of applying it, as Scripture does, to the body, they apply it to the soul. Soul-sleep is nowhere taught in the Bible and is therefore an invention by those who handle the word deceitfully.

[2] *Our Hope*, February, 1902.

WHO WILL BE CAUGHT UP WHEN THE LORD COMES?

The doctrine of the first resurrection and the coming of the Lord for His saints is nowhere taught in the Old Testament; it is altogether a New Testament revelation. As it is so well known, the Apostle Paul, who received from the Lord the revelation concerning the church, the one body, received also directly from the Lord the revelation concerning the glorious removal of the church from the earth. As the church had a definite beginning, so she will have a definite end. This end of the church on earth is made known in 1 Thess. iv: 13-17. To read these familiar words and meditate on them, as we have already done in the preceding chapter, and to realize a little of what it all means, fills the heart with praise and joy unspeakable. Oh, for that shout, that assembling shout from the glorified Head to His own members! The dead in Christ shall rise first, then we which are alive shall be caught up together with them in clouds. The clouds will be the chariots of glory which take us into His presence. Then we shall meet the Lord in the air, and so shall we ever be with the Lord. This coming of the Lord for his saints is the blessed Hope, the Hope of the Church, our Hope.

We are to occupy ourselves next with the question, who, when the hour arrives, will be caught up to meet the Lord in the air. Will all true Christians be caught up or only a few? This is an important question, important because that blessed event may come at any time. There is, in our days, a decided increase of teachers who teach what has been termed a "partial rapture." According to some of these teachings only those who believe that the Lord is coming, and who wait for His coming, who have a correct knowledge of His Second Coming, will be taken, and others who had not light on dispensational teachings, but were equally sincere, will be left to pass through the tribulation. Others again declare that only those will be caught up who attained to a certain spirituality. What is termed "a higher life experience" is, according to these, necessary to share in the rapture. Only "consecrated" Christians will be taken up who are loosened from earthly things. This teaching is found mostly among Christian believers, who are much occupied with themselves, their experiences, and who do not know the blessed position the believer holds through grace in Christ. Then there are numerous groups of people, some of them perfectionists, who are scattered from Maine to California, from North to South and who claim that only the 144,000 will be caught up, and that those who hold these teachings, or, possess their peculiar experience, will belong to that company. These people forget that the 144,000 in Revelation are of Israel. Some of the so-called "Pentecostal people," now split up in different sects, have imposed another condition, that of speaking in a strange tongue. There is still another view, or rather new presentation of the partial rapture, which seems to have unsettled some believers. We have received a number of letters from students and others have come to us and asked us about it.

According to this view only those will have part in the first resurrection whose love and conduct after their conversion have made them worthy of it. We shall quote from a volume which teaches this:

"By the first resurrection Christ exercises His power; when, as we shall presently see, those only, whose love and conduct after conversion have caused Him to deem them worthy, will come forth from the dead, to form the complete church and to act as members of the Heavenly Kingdom.

"By the final resurrection of all the remaining dead; when those who have been saved, but did not attain to the First resurrection, will be raised to life: and those who have rejected the Saviour will come forth for judgment. This resurrection does not take place until the close of the millennial reign, that is, until at least a thousand years after the First resurrection."

According to this the first resurrection is a reward for faithfulness and right conduct. One has to attain a worthiness, what measure of it is not specified, and could not be specified by anyone. The complete church will be formed by those who are faithful. The other believers who were truly saved, and also indwelt by the Holy Spirit, but less faithful, will see no resurrection till the great White Throne is set up. That this is altogether unscriptural need not to be further explained. No believer, who is saved by grace and hence is a member of Christ, will ever appear before the great White Throne. The second resurrection is of the wicked dead.

The author then goes to the Epistle to the Philippians and tries to show from the third chapter that the first resurrection is a prize. Especially is it the word of the Apostle in the tenth and eleventh verses he explains as supporting his false theory. We will let him speak in his own words:

"But what was the goal towards which Paul was thus directing his efforts? 'If by any means,' he continues, 'I may attain to the select resurrection out from among the dead.' In other words, his aim was to be numbered with those blessed and holy ones who shall have part in the first resurrection. But we must note, that he had at the time, *no certain assurance* (italics ours) that he would compass the desire of his heart. * * * Just before his death, however, it was graciously revealed to him that he was one of the approved."

Speaking on the thirteenth and fourteenth verses of the same chapter in Philippians, he says:

"Here Paul again urges the fact, that, devoted as he was to his Master, he had as yet *no absolute certainty* of attaining to the first resurrection."

The worst statement on this line in the whole book is the following:

"The upward, or heavenward, calling is, of course, contrasted with the earthly calling of Israel. And its introduction here is sufficiently startling for those who have been taught that simple belief in Christ will win heaven for them, and membership in the Lord's body. For Paul unmistakably affirms that these high privileges are a prize and not a gift, and are accessible only by the gate of the First Resurrection—a gate through which, after all his sacrifices and labors and sufferings for Christ, he was not yet absolutely sure that he would be permitted to pass."

According to this teaching the Apostle, who had received apostleship not of men but from the Lord, whom he saw in glory, the Apostle to whom was committed the Gospel of the Glory of the blessed God and to whom was made known the mystery of the Church, and that *all* believers are members of that body, this great Apostle and instrument through

28

whom God gave the greatest revelation, did not know himself that he belonged to the body. He did not know it in spite of his sufferings and labors; he had to suffer some more, and only when he wrote Second Timothy had he a special revelation that he had labored and suffered enough. How ridiculous and more than that, insulting to the work and the Word of our Lord Jesus Christ! And if it were true what this book teaches, how dreadful it would be for almost every believer, for but few, if any, labor and suffer as Paul did, and we could have, even if we did, no assurance concerning our membership in the body and our share in the first resurrection, except by *special* revelation. But such a special revelation is nowhere promised in the Word.

We shall return after a while to the argument of Philippians.

But let us give the answer to the question, "*Who will be caught up when the Lord comes?*"

Every person who fell asleep in Jesus belongs to the company which is mentioned in first Thessalonians, "the dead in Christ shall be raised first," and every true believer in the Lord Jesus Christ, who lives when the assembling shout comes from the air, will be caught up in clouds to meet the Lord in the air. And if believers, as it is the case, were ignorant of the coming of the Lord, had absolutely no knowledge of the fact and therefore did not wait for Him, they will nevertheless be caught up. Let us make the statement as strong as we possibly can. Supposing the Lord came tonight to take His own out of the earth. Let us suppose a person who lived a very wicked life, but an hour before the Lord comes believes in the Lord Jesus Christ and is saved and accepted in the Beloved, made a partaker of the heavenly calling. This one saved by grace, though ignorant of the truth of God, would be caught up like the oldest, most matured Saint who loved His appearing for many years. Think of the dying thief. He pleaded "Remember me when thou dost come into thy kingdom." The assurance comes back to him, who could do no works to gain a prize, who was so ignorant in all spiritual matters, "To-day thou shalt be with me in Paradise." When the Lord comes with the assembling shout the body of the thief, saved by grace, as well as the body of Stephen, whose is a martyr's crown, and Paul's and every other one who was saved by grace will be raised up and we, meaning every saved one together with them, will be caught up.

But let us prove this statement by the only authority we have, the Word of God. Let the Scriptures give an answer to the simple question, "Is the first resurrection and to be caught up to meet the Lord in the air the prize for a holy, consecrated, faithful conduct and life, or is it a free gift of the grace of God in our Lord Jesus Christ?" The answer to this from the Scriptures is clear; it is put in every epistle as the result of grace and not as the reward for faithfulness and service. To cite all the New Testament passages which acquaint us with the wonderful truth of what grace has called us to and made us in Christ Jesus would fill page after page, and if we would ponder over them and search in its blessed depths under the guidance of the Holy Spirit, would fill our hearts with "joy unspeakable and full of glory." How clear it is seen in *Romans*. In the fifth of Romans we read of the blessed results of justification. It is not a question of *doing* from our side, but it is *God's doing*, for everyone who believeth on the Lord Jesus Christ. Peace, perfect peace, towards God. Every believer has it with God in virtue of the blood of the cross. There peace was made. The second, access by faith into this grace, wherein we stand, and the third result of justification, rejoicing in hope of the glory of God. And this hope of the glory of God is nothing else than what we have in the first epistle of John, "We shall be like Him for we shall see Him as He is." Read also Romans viii:29, 30, "For whom He did foreknow, He also did predestinate to be conformed to the image of His Son (in resurrection on the day of His coming for His Saints) that He might be the Firstborn among many brethren. Moreover, whom He did predestinate, them He also called, and whom He called, them He also justified and whom He justified, them He also glorified." Justification and glorification are inseparably connected. They cannot be severed. Both are from the side of God, the result of the finished work of our Lord Jesus Christ. God has justified and God has glorified. The glorification begins when our Lord leaves the Father's throne and comes into the air to meet those whom the Father has given to Him. Not one will be left behind. And who are they whom the Father has given to the Son? Everyone who believed and came to the Son.

It is in that rich unfathomable epistle to the Ephesians, where we read God's gracious purpose towards everyone who believes in Christ, accepted in Him, blest with all spiritual blessings in the heavenlies in Christ. We would have to go through all the precious words in the opening chapters, where we learn more fully than elsewhere that *it is all the gift of God*, not of works, lest any man should boast. "Even when we were dead in sins hath quickened us together with Christ (by grace ye are saved). And hath raised us up together and made us sit together in the heavenlies in Christ Jesus; that in the ages to come He might show the exceeding riches of His grace in kindness toward us through Christ Jesus." Now we are there by grace. God see us there in Christ and bye and bye we shall be there actually. It is clear from a number of passages that when the Lord comes for His Saints *all* believers without any distinction, whether they are full grown in knowledge, fathers, young men or babes in Christ, will be taken *because* they are Christ's and God's grace has put them there. This is not only clearly seen in 1 Thess. iv:13-18, but also elsewhere. "For our commonwealth is in heaven, from whence also we look for the Savior, the Lord Jesus Christ; Who shall change our body of humiliation, that it might be fashioned like unto His glorious body, according to the working whereby He is able even to subdue all things unto Himself" (Phil. iii:20, 21). But every man in his own order: Christ the first fruits; afterwards *they that are Christ's* at His coming, * * * Behold, I shew you a mystery; we shall not all sleep, but we shall *all* be changed (1 Cor. xv:23, 51). It is clear that *all* means the whole company of believers.

But there are other scriptural proofs that all believers will be taken up when the Lord comes. One is the unity of the body. "For as the body is one and hath many members, and all the members of that one body, being many, are one body; so also is Christ. For by one Spirit are we *all* baptised into *one* body" (1 Cor. xii:12 and 13). It is clear then that all believers are members of the one body. The teaching in the above cited paragraphs is an open denial of the truth revealed of the church as the one body. "There is *one* body and *one* Spirit even as ye are called in *one* hope of your calling" (Ephes. iv:4). This one body, of which every believer is a member, will be joined to the glorified Head, it will be *one* joining and one presentation of the assembly. Now, if only certain believers are caught up and another number passeth through a part of the tribulation, and still another company is taken later and other believers will not be raised at all till the great white Throne is set up, the revealed truth of the one body, its organic unity and vital connection with Him in glory is completely set aside.

Furthermore, *the* apostasy and the revelation of the Antichrist cannot come till that body, the church, is taken from the earth (see 2 Thess. ii). The appearance of the final Antichrist therefore demands the complete removal of the one body. A remnant of believers, members of the one body, left in the earth during the great tribulation would still hinder the revelation of Antichrist and postpone it. The Saints in the tribulation are *not* members of the one body, but they are Jewish believers. The next chapter will enter into this more fully.

Again, "We must all appear before the judgment seat of Christ." This is the *Bema* in the air. *All* believers will have to appear before Him to receive approval or disapproval (*not* salvation or condemnation). Now, if they are *all* to appear before that seat in the air on the day of Christ— they must *all* have been taken up. When He comes at the end of the tribulation He comes with *all* His Saints. Many other Scriptures might be quoted which declare the same truth, Every believer will share in the first resurrection and be caught up when the Lord comes.

31

There are two passages which are generally quoted to support the teaching of a partial rapture. The first is taken to support the theory that it is a question of worthiness, and the second passage is claimed to make clear that only those will be caught up who look for the Lord.

Luke xxi:36 is the first passage. "Watch ye therefore and pray always, that ye may be accounted worthy to escape all the things that shall come to pass and to stand before the Son of Man." Our Lord spoke these words in connection with the prophecies concerning the end of the age when the earth and the heavens shall be shaken and when He will come as Son of Man in a cloud with power and glory. The title of our Lord, Son of Man, gives us His relation to the earth. When He was here in His humiliation He was Son of Man, when He comes in exaltation He comes as Son of Man. Nowhere is it said of the members of the body of the Lord Jesus Christ that they will stand before the Son of Man. The exhortation is one which concerns the Jewish remnant, the 144,000 in the Book of Revelation. They will be in the earth during that time of trouble and with them it will be the question of faithfulness to the end to be accounted worthy to stand before the Son of Man. The disciples whom our Lord addressed in these words represent in type that Jewish remnant.

Hebrews ix:28: "So Christ was once offered to bear the sins of many; and unto them that look for Him shall He appear the second time without sin unto salvation." This passage has been made to prove that only those who wait for Him will be taken up. The whole passage shows the three appearings of the Christ. He appeared on the earth to put away sin by sacrificing Himself. He appears now in the presence of God for us. He will appear the second time. This is unquestionably the glorious appearing spoken of in Titus ii:13, "The glorious appearing of the great God and our Saviour Jesus Christ." *He* who appeared and *He* who appears in the presence of God will be the *same* who comes back to the earth. Of course when He actually returns from heaven into the habitable earth, as the firstborn, bringing many sons to glory (all His saints with Him) there will be such who wait and look for Him and to them He comes for salvation, and these are the believing Jews. Of this we read in Isaiah xxv:9: "And it shall be said in that day, Lo this is our God; we have waited for Him and He will save us. This is the Lord; we have waited for Him, we will be glad and rejoice in His salvation." The passage does not teach that only such will be caught up who believe in His coming and look for Him.

And now, as so many believers seem to be troubled about the words of the Apostle Paul in the third chapter of Philippians we give a short word on that. The position of the epistle to the Philippians is significant. Ephesians speaks of the glories of the church, what every believer and the company of believers, the one body, is *in* Christ. Colossians acquaints us with the glory of Him who is the Head of the body, Christ. Philippians stands between the two and shows the believer in Christ with the life of Christ in him, living Christ and pressing towards the glory. It is the epistle of experience. In the third chapter the energy of this life in the believer is seen. Paul, of course, knew that he belonged to that glory. He had absolute certainty about the first resurrection. But this divine energy in him presses forward. It is in full harmony with what God's grace has made him. All in him wants to get there, where the grace of God in Christ had placed him once and for all. The life of Christ in him reaches out for that place and when he says, "By any means," he gives us to understand nothing shall hinder him, may the cost be what it will, he wants to lay hold of all for which Christ has laid hold of him. He reaches out after that goal, Christ in glory, because he knew he belonged there.

Sir Robert Anderson gives a very helpful comment on Philippians iii:11 which we quote in connection with the above:

"If the commonly received exegesis of this passage be correct, we are faced by the astounding fact that the author of the Epistle to the Romans and of the fifteenth chapter of 1 Corinthians—the Apostle who was in a peculiar sense entrusted with the supreme revelation of grace—announced when nearing the close of his ministry that the resurrection was not, as he had been used to teach, a blessing which Divine grace assured to all believers in Christ, but a prize to be won by the sustained efforts of a life of wholly exceptional saintship.

"Nor is this all. In the same Epistle he has already said, 'To me to live is Christ, and to die is gain,' whereas, *ex hypothesi*, it now appears that his chief aim was to earn a right to the resurrection, and that death, instead of bringing gain, would have cut him off before he had reached the standard of saintship needed to secure that prize! For his words are explicit. 'Not as though I had already attained.'

"Here was one who was not a whit behind the chiefest Apostles; who excelled them all in labors and sufferings for his Lord, and in the visions and revelations accorded to him; whose prolonged ministry, moreover, was accredited by mighty signs and wonders, by the power of the spirit of God. And yet, being now 'such an one as Paul the aged,' he was in doubt whether he should have part in that resurrection which he had taught all his Corinthian converts to hope for and expect.

"Such is the exposition of the Apostle's teaching in many a standard commentary. And yet the passage which is thus perverted reaches its climax in the words, 'Our citizenship is in heaven, from whence we are looking for the Savior, the Lord Jesus Christ, who shall fashion anew the body of our humiliation that it may be conformed to the body of His glory.'

"'Our citizenship is in heaven.' Here is the clew to the teaching of the whole passage. The truth to which his words refer is more clearly stated in Ephesians ii:6, 'God has quickened us together with Christ, and raised us up with Him, and made us sit with Him in the heavenly places in Christ.' More clearly still is it given in Colossians iii:1-3, 'If then ye were raised together with Christ, seek the things that are above, where Christ is, seated on the right hand of God. Set your mind on the things that are above, not on the things on the earth. For ye died, and your life is hid with Christ in God.'

"Ephesians and Colossians, be it remembered, were written at the same period of his ministry as Philippians, and in the light of these Scriptures we can read this chapter aright. To win Christ (v. 8), or to apprehend, or lay hold of, that for which he had been laid hold of, or apprehended (v. 12)—or in other words, to realize practically in his life on earth what was true of him doctrinally as to his standing before God in heaven—this is what he was reaching toward, and what he says he had not already attained.

"The high calling of verse 14 is interpreted by some to mean Christ's calling up His own to meet Him in the air (a blessing assured to all 'who are alive and remain unto the Coming of the Lord'), but this is not in keeping with the plain words: God's high calling in Christ Jesus, *i. e.*, what God has called us (made us) to be in Christ.

"If the passage refers to the literal resurrection, then the words, 'not as though I had already attained,' must mean that, while here on earth and before the Lord's Coming, the Apostle hoped either to undergo the change of verse 21, or else to win some sort of saintship diploma, or certificate, to ensure his being raised at the Coming. These alternatives are inexorable; and they only need to be stated to ensure their rejection.

"One word more. If the Apostle Paul, after such a life of saintship and service, was in doubt as to his part in the resurrection, no one of us, indeed he be the proudest of Pharisees or the blindest of fools, will dream of attaining it."

THE CHURCH AND THE GREAT TRIBULATION

Nothing should unite God's children into a closer fellowship than the blessed hope of the coming of our Lord. This was the case, when the Holy Spirit, almost a hundred years ago, restored to His people this hope, and brought about a revival of the study of prophecy. The midnight cry,

"Behold the Bridegroom! Go ye forth to meet Him," was then sounded, and those who heard and believed the blessed hope separated themselves from all which is not according to sound doctrine, and in so doing manifested once more the oneness of the body of Christ, the church, and the fellowship of the Saints. Such ought to be the results of a real faith in His coming.

One of the questions which has agitated believers in the premillennial Coming of our Lord is the question of the relation of the true church to that final period of our age, which is designated as the great tribulation. When the blessed hope was first again brought to light, clear distinction was made between the Coming of the Lord for His Saints (1 Thess. iv:13-18) and the Coming of the Lord with His Saints (Zech. xiv:5; Rev. xix:14). The imminency of His Coming was a prominent part of the prophetic testimony of those bygone days. Then the teaching was introduced by some that the Lord cannot come at any time, that the church is destined to pass, like the rest of the world, through the great tribulation, suffer under Antichrist and experience the judgment-wrath of God. This theory has caused much division and strife among believers in the Return of our Lord, and does so still.

In taking up this question concerning the church and the tribulation, we shall first see what the church and the destiny of the church is, and then examine the teaching of the Word as to the tribulation.

I. What is the Church and the Destiny of the Church?

The church is an altogether New Testament institution. Nowhere in the Old Testament Scriptures is there said anything about the church, the expression so often used, the Old Testament church, or, the Jewish church is therefore incorrect. It springs from the view that Israel, the seed of Abraham, was the church in the past and that since Israel has rejected Christ, the Christian Church has become Israel and all the promises made to Israel are now being fulfilled in a spiritual way. This theory plays havoc with the Word of God and leads into confusion. The presentday condition of Christendom is to a great extent the result of this erroneous view. Israel is not the church, nor has the church taken the place of Israel. All who believed in Old Testament times were saved by grace, in the same way as believing sinners are saved during this dispensation. They were Saints, as we are Saints. But where is there in any portion of the Scriptures of the Old Testament (so-called) a statement that these Jewish believers formed the church of God, the body and the bride of Christ? Israel was not the church in the past and it is equally impossible that the people Israel in their future day of restoration and blessing can

35

become the church. Israel's calling is earthly; the calling of the church is a heavenly calling. Israel will some day possess the earthly Jerusalem while the church will be in the heavenly Jerusalem.

Our Lord mentioned the church for the first time. In the Gospel of Matthew xvi:16-18 we find the following words:

"And Simon Peter answered and said, Thou art the Christ, the Son of the living God. And Jesus answered and said unto him, Blessed art thou, Simon Bar-Jona: for flesh and blood hath not revealed it unto thee, but my Father which is in heaven. And I say also unto thee, That thou art Peter, and upon this rock I will build my church; and the gates of hell shall not prevail against it."

Peter had made his great inspired confession of Christ as the Son of the living God. Upon this confession the Lord said, "Blessed art thou, Simon Bar-Jona." Each believer in the Lord Jesus Christ as the Son of God shares this blessedness. He called Simon by a new name, "Thou art Peter;" which means "a stone." Then the Lord announced that upon this rock He would build His church. He did not mean Peter, or else our Lord would have said, "Upon thee will I build my church." He speaks of "this rock" which is He Himself, the risen and living Son of God. He, and not Peter, is the rock upon which the Church of Christ is built. We see that the Lord speaks of the church as something in the future at that time. It was not then in progress, but He said, "I *will* build my church." The word church means "to call out" (ecclesia), and denotes a company of people who are called out and called together for a certain purpose. The Lord calls this outcalled company "my church." The formation of this church could only begin after the work of redemption on the cross had been accomplished. He had first to suffer and to die; He had to rise from the dead and ascend upon high; the Holy Spirit had to come from heaven before this church and its building could begin on earth. Therefore He said "I will build my church;" not I am building it now, or it has been building since Adam's day, but "I *will* build."

The day on which the Holy Spirit was poured out marks the beginning of this church on earth. The company of believers who were waiting for the promised baptism with the Spirit (about 120-Acts i:15) were on the day of Pentecost by that baptism united into a body, the church. Ever since then all who believe on the Lord Jesus Christ and are born again, are put by the same spirit as members into that body. Of this we read in 1 Cor. xii:13: "For by our Spirit are we all baptized into one body, whether we be Jews or Gentiles, whether we be bond or free, and have been all made to drink into one Spirit." On the day of Pentecost nothing was made known of the beginning of the church. Peter did not mention a

36

word about the church. The full revelation concerning the church was given through the Apostle Paul. Of this we read in Ephes. iii:1-7:

"For this cause I, Paul, the prisoner of Jesus Christ for you Gentiles, if ye have heard of the dispensation of the grace of God which is given me to you ward; how that by revelation he made known unto me the mystery (as I wrote afore in few words, whereby, when ye read, ye may understand my knowledge in the mystery of Christ), which in other ages was not made known unto the sons of men, as it is now revealed unto his holy apostles and prophets by the Spirit; that the Gentiles should be fellowheirs, and of the same body, and partakers of his promise in Christ by the gospel; whereof I was made a minister, according to the gift of the grace of God given unto me by the effectual working of his power."

The Apostle Paul states in these verses that he was made the channel of a revelation concerning a mystery which was not made known in former ages unto the sons of men. This mystery is that the Gentiles should be fellowheirs, and of the same body. The body of which he speaks, is the church. In that body Jews and Gentiles are gathered into one, as the one new man "where there is neither Greek nor Jew, circumcision nor uncircumcision, barbarian, Scythian, bond nor free, but Christ is all and in all." Of this bringing into one we read in the Gospel of John (chapter x) where our Lord spoke of entering the sheepfold (Judaism) and leading out His sheep. Then He mentioned other sheep, which were not of His fold (Gentiles): "Them also I must bring, and they shall hear my voice, and there shall be one flock and one shepherd." He came and led His first sheep out of the Jewish fold. On the day of Pentecost these Jewish believers were constituted the Church. That Gentiles should be added to that body was not made known then. It was revealed to the Apostle Paul. But the Lord indicates this fact here when He speaks of the other sheep. This He mentioned likewise in His prayer: "That they all (who believe on Him) may be one; as Thou, Father, art in me, and I in Thee, that they also may be one in us, that the world may believe that thou hast sent me" (John xvii:21). The Epistle to the Ephesians, in which the Spirit of God reveals this mystery, makes known the glory of the church, the body of Christ. He is the head of that body and as such the church is His own fulness, "the fulness of Him who filleth all in all" (Eph. i:23). Every member in that body shares the life of the risen, glorified head. Every member is quickened together with Christ, raised up and seated in the heavenlies in Christ Jesus (ii:5-6). And furthermore we read that the members of this body, that is, all true believers, saved by grace and born again, are made nigh by the blood of Christ, and have access by one Spirit unto the Father. "Now, therefore, ye are no more strangers and foreigners, but fellow-citizens with the saints, and of the household of

God; and are built upon the foundation of the apostles and prophets, Jesus Christ Himself being the chief cornerstone; in whom all the building fitly framed together groweth unto an holy temple in the Lord. In whom ye also are builded together for an habitation of God through the Spirit" (ii:19-22). Such is the church the body of Christ. Every member in Christ and Christ in every member, each believer made nigh by blood, accepted in the beloved One, indwelt by the Holy Spirit and one Spirit with the Lord. The church is therefore the temple of God, the habitation of God through the Spirit.

Besides this life-relation of the church to the Head in glory, there is also a love-relation. Of this Ephesians v:21-33 bears witness. The church is the bride of Christ. He loved the church and gave Himself for it. She is part of that travail of His soul which He saw, the joy which was set before Him, for which He endured the cross and despised the shame. He also sanctifies the church and cleanseth it with the washing of water by the Word, and finally He will present it to Himself a glorious church, not having spot or wrinkle, or any such thing, but that it should be holy and without blemish. She is the pearl of great price for which He gave all. Her destiny is to be with Him in glory, to be like Him and to share His glory. For this true church there is no condemnation and no wrath, nor anguish and tribulation, but glory, honor and peace (Rom. ii:9-10). Wrath is coming for the world, but the Lord Jesus delivers His church from the wrath to come (1 Thess. i:10). "For God hath not appointed us to wrath, but to obtain salvation by our Lord Jesus Christ" (1 Thess. v:9).

II. What is the Tribulation?

The Word of God speaks of tribulation. Tribulations, distresses and all that goes with it are in the world on account of sin. Believers, though saved and no longer of the world, but delivered from this evil age, have tribulation and persecution likewise. Our Lord said to His disciples and to all who are His followers, "In the world ye shall have tribulation, but be of good cheer, I have overcome the world" (John xvi:33). "If they have persecuted me, they will also persecute you" (John xv:20). "Yea, and all that will live godly in Christ Jesus shall suffer persecution" (1 Tim. 12). What a record Paul wrote of his own tribulations and persecutions. How great was his affliction, persecution, distress and manifold tribulation! (2 Cor. xi:16-32). "Through much tribulation we must enter into the Kingdom of God" (Acts xiv:22). The believer is exhorted to glory (or boast) in these tribulations (Rom. v:3). Triumphantly in faith he can say, "Who shall separate us, from the love of Christ? Shall tribulation, or distress, or persecution, or famine, or nakedness, or peril, or sword?" (Rom. viii:35). "Rejoicing in hope, patient in tribulation," is another exhortation (Rom. xii:12). To the Corinthians Paul wrote, "I am filled with comfort, I am exceeding joyful in all our tribulation" (2 Cor. vii:4). The Thessalonian Christians suffered greatly, but met it all victoriously so that Paul wrote them, "We ourselves glory in you in the churches of God for your patience and faith in all your persecutions and tribulations that ye endure" (1 Thess. i:4). If we today know but little persecution for Christ's sake, it is because we do not manifest in our lives separation from the world. "For unto you it is given in the behalf of Christ, not only to believe on Him, but also to suffer for His sake" (Phil. i:29). Tribulations, persecutions, sufferings for Christ's and for righteousness' sake belong to the church. They are really blessings, for all these things must work together for good to them that love God.

But there is another tribulation revealed in the Word of God which is of totally different nature. It is a tribulation which God permits as a judgment to come upon all the world, a tribulation in which Satan is concerned, in which he manifests his malice and his wrath. This tribulation has an altogether punitive character. In different portions of the Prophets we read of a great time of distress, such as the sword, famine and pestilence and other tribulations and judgments, which precede the visible manifestation of the Lord to deliver His earthly people Israel. This tribulation is always predicted to come upon Israel and upon the nations of the earth. It is mentioned in the New Testament, as we shall see directly; but the Old Testament gives us the full history of these tribulation judgments. The time when this tribulation takes place is "the end of the age," which, strictly speaking means the Jewish age. Every student of prophecy knows something of that all important revelation in Daniel ix, the seventy-week prophecy.[1]

The last prophetic week of seven years has not yet been. We are still between the 69th and the 70th week. Those coming last seven years of that interrupted Jewish age will bring these predicted judgments and the great tribulation. The last 3-1/2 years (or 1,260 days, 42 months) are the great tribulation itself.

We quote a few passages: "Alas! for that day is great, so that none is like it, it is even the time of Jacob's trouble, but he shall be saved out of it" (Jer. xxx-7).

"And at that time shall Michael stand up, the great prince who standeth for the children of thy people; and there shall be a time of trouble, such as never was since there was a nation even to that same time. And at that time thy people shall be delivered, every one that shall be found written in the book" (Dan. xii:1).

39

It is clear beyond controversy that both passages reveal that this great time of trouble comes upon Daniel's people at the time of the end. It is a wrong interpretation to say that "thy people" means the church. As stated before, the prophets have nothing to say about the church. For what will take place in that time of trouble see Dan. vii:21-25. We turn next to Matthew xxiv. The great prophecy of our Lord contained in this chapter has nothing to do with the destruction of Jerusalem in 70 A. D. It is a prophecy which relates to the time of the end and covers the same seven years of unfulfilled Jewish history. His disciples had asked concerning the end of the age and the Lord answers this question. Significant it is that He calls special attention to Daniel the prophet. This is the key. When our Lord speaks of a time of trouble He means the same trouble of which Daniel wrote: "For there shall be great tribulation such as was not since the beginning of the world to this time, no nor ever shall be" (Matt. xxiv:21). There is nothing in the words of our Lord to indicate that the true church is then on earth. The preaching of the Gospel of the Kingdom as a witness to all nations during this time of trouble is the message which the Jewish remnant gives before the coming of the King.[2] When this great tribulation ends the Lord Jesus Christ comes back to earth again "in the clouds of heaven with power and great glory" (Matt. xxiv:29-30). What takes place then is revealed also by our Lord. "And He shall send His angels with a great sound of a trumpet, and they shall gather together His elect from the four winds, from one end of heaven to the other." Superficial teachers of prophecy explain this as being the gathering together of Christian believers when the Lord comes at the close of the great tribulation. We have seen from 1 Thess. iv:13-18 how the Lord comes for His Saints. He does not send angels to gather His church from the four winds, but He gives the shout from the air and instead of being gathered the church-saints are caught up in clouds, together with the risen saints to meet the Lord in the air. The elect people who are to be gathered when the Lord returns after the tribulation are the people Israel (see Isaiah xxvii:13). Their hour of deliverance has come. This is the same deliverance of which Daniel speaks in chapter xii:1. It is also significant that our Lord after He announced the gathering and restoration of Israel mentions at once the figtree, which is Israel.

The book of Revelation bears the same witness as to the church and in relation to the tribulation to come. The church is only mentioned in the first three chapters. In the church message to Philadelphia (Rev. iii:7-13) a promise is given to the true church which is important: "Because thou hast kept the word of my patience, I also will keep thee from the hour of trial which shall come upon all the world to try them that dwell upon the earth. Behold I come quickly, hold that fast which thou hast that no man take thy crown." The hour of trial for all the world is the tribulation period. Here, then, is a definite promise that true believers are going to be exempt from that coming time of trouble. Laodicea marks a final phase of Christendom; it is apostasy. Chapters iv and v in Revelation reveal what will take place in heaven in the future. We behold in these two chapters the redeemed in glory, singing the new song. These redeemed include all the church saints as well as the Old Testament Saints. Beginning with the sixth chapter we find in Revelation the future things, that is, what will take place after the Lord has come for His Saints. Here the judgments, the tribulation and the wrath are made known which will visit the earth during the last seven years of the age. Revelation vi-xviii cover the history of the last week of Daniel. In these chapters we read nothing of the true church as still on earth.

Another important fact as to the tribulation period must be dealt with. During this time of trouble there are those on earth who suffer and whom God owns as Saints. Satan through his instruments, the little horn and the Antichrist is persecuting these Saints and they pass through this awful time of trouble. Daniel wrote, "I beheld, and the same horn made war with the Saints and prevailed against them ... and he (the little horn) shall speak great words against the Most High and shall wear out the Saints of the Most High" (Daniel vii:21, 25). These suffering tribulation Saints will receive the Kingdom on earth (Dan. vii:22, 27). In the great vision of John in Revelation chapter xiii, the same beast which Daniel saw is described. Here again we read of Saints: "And it was given unto him to make war with the Saints, and to overcome them" (Rev. xiii:7). Now as the church is no longer on earth, who are these Saints? They are Jewish believers who have turned to the Lord and whom He now owns as Saints. Their sufferings at that time, as well as their faith, their prayers and their deliverance is the subject of many of the Psalms. They are the sealed ones of Revelation vii.[3] Many of them refusing to worship the beast suffer martyrdom and are raised up.

III. Important Conclusions

We have seen what the church and her destiny is. We have learned the character of the tribulation. It is evident that the true church has nothing whatever to do with this time of trouble. We add some important conclusions with further proofs that the church will not pass through the tribulation.

1. The tribulation is a judgment period. When this predicted trouble comes for the world, for Jews and Gentiles, the church is no longer here, but possesses its promised rest and glory. The Thessalonians had been

disturbed by a rumor as if that tribulation preceding the day of the Lord had come. In the second Epistle to them the apostle makes it clear that this was not the case, and points out the fact that those who troubled and persecuted them would have as a recompense tribulation, while the troubled believers would have rest (2 Thess. i:4-9). Nowhere in the Epistles of Paul addressed to the church, and unfolding church truths, is there a word said about that tribulation. If the church would pass through this judgment period with which the ages closes, the Spirit of God would certainly have mentioned it and given His exhortations so suited for such a time. But inasmuch as nothing is said in these church epistles it is a logical conclusion that the true church will not be in the tribulation.

2. Not alone will the church not be in that time of trouble, but that time, the last prophetic week of Daniel, cannot begin as long as the true church is on earth. This is made clear by one of the great prophecies of the New Testament. In the Second Thessalonians chapter ii the statement is made that the day of the Lord (His visible manifestation) cannot come till there be first the apostasy and the Man of Sin, the son of perdition (the Antichrist) be revealed. It is during the last seven years that both of these conditions are reached. But the apostle also states that there is One who hinders the complete apostasy and its leader, the Antichrist. Something is in the way which keeps back the full manifestation of the mystery of lawlessness. This hindering One must be first taken out of the way. The hindering One is the Holy Spirit. He dwells in the body of Christ, the church. As long as He is here on earth in and with the true church the two conditions necessary for the final seven years of this age cannot be fulfilled. Before the tribulation can come the church must have been called away to her heavenly abode.

3. If the church were to pass through the tribulation period all the exhortations to wait for the Coming of the Lord, to watch for Him, to be ready, would have no meaning. It would be more correct to exhort to wait for the coming of the beast. The blessed hope to meet Him, would lose its blessedness. Instead of being a bright outlook to be with Christ in glory, it would be the worst pessimism, for believers would not face immediate glory, but tribulation, judgments, and the persecutions of the beast from the pit. Everything in Scripture is against this teaching, which has been accepted by not a few, that the church must pass through the tribulation, and after all it is an important truth for the spiritual life of a believer. If the Lord cannot come for His Saints till the Roman empire is again in existence, and the two beasts have made their appearance to do their work, if He cannot come till the Jews are back in Palestine and have rebuilt their temple, then the real power of that blessed hope in the daily

42

life of a Christian is gone. The danger then is to say, "My Lord delays His Coming," and with it drift into worldly ways.

[1] See "Exposition of Daniel," by A. C. G.

[2] See chapter on "The Conversion of the World."

[3] In Rev. vii a multitude is seen coming out of the great tribulation. This multitude is often identified with the church. But it is not the church, but those who believe the final testimony, the Gospel of the kingdom and are saved to enter the earth by the Kingdom of Christ.

<h1 style="text-align:center">THE TEN VIRGINS</h1>

or

<h1 style="text-align:center">THE MIDNIGHT CRY</h1>

Matthew xxv:1-13

The study of this most solemn parable spoken by our Lord is very opportune. It is also necessary because certain wrong interpretations are being made of this parable, which have been accepted by not a few of God's people.

We find the parable of the ten virgins exclusively in the Gospel of Matthew, and here it is a part of the great discourse of our Lord, generally known as the Olivet discourse. The Gospel of Matthew is the Gospel of the King and His Kingdom. Three great discourses of the Lord are recorded by the Holy Spirit in the Gospel of Matthew. The first is the so-called "sermon on the mount." This contains the proclamation of the King concerning His Kingdom. The second discourse is found in the 13th chapter; this is composed of seven parables in which the Lord makes known the mysteries of the Kingdom. In the last great discourse He reveals the future of His Kingdom. First He reveals the future of the Jews, how the Jewish age will close, what great events are yet to take place in the land of Israel. He speaks of the great tribulation, which is yet in store for the Jews and immediately after the days of that great tribulation He will come in power and great glory. At the close of His discourse He reveals the future of the Gentile nations, who are on earth when He comes again. He will take His place upon His own glorious throne and all nations will be gathered before Him. They will be separated by the King, as a shepherd separates the sheep and the goats. Between these two predictions concerning the future, the beginning and the end of this discourse He gives three parables. These parables do not relate to the Jews, nor to the Gentile nations nor do they refer to the

43

period of time, the end of the age, of which He speaks in the first part of Matthew xxiv. In these three parables the Lord shows the conditions which will prevail during the time of His absence from this earth. *This period of time is the present Christian age.* The three parables of the prudent and evil servant, the wise and the foolish virgins and the faithful and the slothful servants, give us a picture of the state of the entire Christian profession. This is seen in the very beginning of this parable. The parable of the ten virgins is one, which relates to the kingdom of heaven. The kingdom of heaven has here the same meaning as in Matthew xiii, that is, it means the entire sphere of Christian profession.

And now before we follow the different stages of this important parable I want to mention very briefly the two wrong interpretations, which like all other errors in our day, became more and more widespread. The first claims that the virgins do not represent Christians at all, but that they represent the Jewish remnant during the end of the age. The parable, according to this interpretation, will be fulfilled in the future. I am not going to enter into the different arguments which are advanced to support this view, but only wish to point out one fact, which is sufficient to disprove this theory. The ten virgins fell asleep, which, as we shall see later, means that they no longer expected the coming of the Bridegroom. Is it possible to conceive that the believing Jews during the great tribulation, when everything points to the rapid consummation of the age, can go to sleep? This to my mind is sufficient to overthrow this theory, not to speak of other reasons.

Another interpretation holds that the ten virgins represent indeed Christians. However, the foolish virgins are looked upon as true Christians, only they lacked a maturity of growth, depth of consecration, were not baptized with the Holy Spirit, or had not the so-called "second blessing." All this the wise virgins possessed. This is the favoured view with a certain class of holiness people. Others try to prove from it the theory of a first fruit rapture. The wise virgins are the first fruits and they are taken first. The foolish will have to pass through the tribulation and will be taken later. Against such teaching we simply hold up the words of the Lord, when He as Bridegroom tells the foolish virgins "I know you not." They were never His, they never knew Him and therefore they do not represent true Christians. Never will the Lord say this word to any one who has truly trusted in Him, no matter how weak and ignorant, how imperfect and erring that one may be.

And now let us look at the details of this parable, which gives us a picture of the attitude and character of professing Christendom up to the time when the Bridegroom comes.

Four historic stages can be easily traced in this parable. Three of them are passed and the fourth is imminent. At any moment the fourth may become actual history. They are the following:

1. A description of the Christian profession in its beginning and its characteristics. 2. The falling asleep of the virgins. 3. The Midnight cry. 4. The Coming of the Bridegroom. We are living in the days when the midnight cry is heard and are facing the fourth great event of this parable, the Coming of the Bridegroom, the entrance of the wise virgins to be with Him and the shutting out of the foolish. And this it is which makes this parable so very solemn in the days in which we are living.

1. "Then shall the kingdom of heaven be likened unto ten virgins, which took their lamps and went forth to meet the Bridegroom." In 2nd Corinthians we read that the virgin is used as a type of the church. "I have espoused you to one husband, that I may present you as a chaste virgin to Christ." The Lord in the parable uses the figure of ten virgins, because the parable does not altogether refer to the true church, His Bride, but because He had in mind the conditions of that which professes to be the church. The number ten is the number of testimony and responsibility. Nevertheless we learn from the beginning of this parable what true Christianity is. The characteristics of the Christian calling are three-fold: separation, manifestation and expectation. Separation from the world; going forth with lamps, which are for giving light, to shine as lights while the Bridegroom is not here; and then to go forth to meet the Bridegroom. One can read in these statements the very words and thoughts with which the Holy Spirit describes the Thessalonian Christians, "How ye turned to God from idols to serve the true and the living God and to wait for His Son from heaven." The emphasis in this parable is upon the last of these characteristics. The whole body of Christians in the beginning went out to meet the Bridegroom. The blessed Hope of the coming of the Lord was the Hope and the expectation of the church in the very start. It was the original attitude of the true church and bears witness to the heavenly hope and heavenly calling of the church.

In the next two verses the spiritual condition of the ten virgins is laid bare. It is noteworthy that the condition is stated first, the demonstration of it comes later; after the midnight cry had been sounded the foolishness of the five becomes manifested. The division of these virgins in five wise and five foolish brings out the fact that in the professing church two classes of people are found, the true and the false, saved and unsaved, professing and possessing. The wise represent such who have believed in the Lord Jesus Christ, who have personal knowledge of Christ and are sealed with the Spirit; they have the unction of the Holy One, who is

45

represented by the oil. The foolish are such who have the form of godliness and deny the power thereof. They represent such who have taken the outward profession but lack the reality. As they never truly trusted in Christ they have not the oil, the Holy Spirit. The objection has been made that the foolish virgins can hardly represent unsaved persons, because they are called virgins and went out to meet the Bridegroom. In their profession they were virgins, and in profession they had gone out to meet the Bridegroom. Another objection is raised. Did they not later say "Give us of your oil, for our lamps are gone out?" Then they must have had some oil, else how could they say that their lamps were gone out? There is no proof at all in this that they had a certain supply of oil. It is distinctly said that they only took lamps, but they did not take oil. They may have made an attempt to light the wick of their lamps only to see that they did not give light and went out. No, they never possessed the oil, just as the great mass of professing Christians in our days have lamps, an outward form, but no reality. Christ was never accepted and therefore the Holy Spirit and His power is lacking. A fearful condition it is! Alas, the thousands and hundreds of thousands who are in that condition to-day!

2. A second stage historically is seen in the fifth verse. "While the Bridegroom tarried, they all slumbered and slept." Both the foolish and the wise grew heavy, became drowsy and then slept. This has been interpreted in different ways. However, the meaning of it is not hard to discover. The Bridegroom tarried and they no longer expected Him. As the centuries went on the professing church gave up the blessed Hope and ceased looking for the Lord. This is an historic fact. The Coming of the Bridegroom was forgotten and all, the most earnest believers as well as the mere professing ones slept, and for long centuries nothing was heard of the Bridegroom and His Coming. Darkness and confusion prevailed in dispensational truths; the writings extending over hundreds of years witness to this fact. Of the end of the world, a universal judgment day, and the Day of wrath something was heard occasionally, but the blessed Hope as it was known in the beginning was completely forgotten. Nothing is heard of it for many, many centuries. This is the second great historic event. The Lord was no longer expected.

3. And now we come to the third. "And at midnight there was a cry made, Behold the Bridegroom! go out to meet Him." The question is has this period been reached, or are we still to wait for such a startling cry, reaching the ears of both the wise and the foolish, the professing and the possessing? Some teach in our day that that cry is the same as the shout which is mentioned in 1 Thess. iv, the shout which the descending Lord will give to call His own into His presence. But that is incorrect. The

midnight cry and the shout of the Lord have no connection. The shout of the Lord is the first word which He will utter. His last word was, "Behold I come quickly." The next word will be His shout. The midnight cry is not uttered by Himself, but it is given by the Holy Spirit. And has the midnight cry been given by the Holy Spirit? Has there been a revival of the blessed Hope of the Coming of the Lord? Did anything like this of which the Lord here speaks take place? We unhesitatingly answer it with, Yes. We all know of the Coming of the Lord. Most of us are cherishing the blessed Hope and are waiting for Himself. We sing precious hymns full of hope and expectation. Over the entire Christian profession the preaching has gone forth of the Coming of the Bridegroom. This is sufficient evidence that this stage in the parable has been reached. The midnight cry has been given. When was it given? We do not hear anything about the Bridegroom and His nearness during the great reformation period. The great instruments which were used in the reformation had no light on the Coming of the Lord. Luther, for instance, spoke occasionally of the great universal judgment day, which he believed was near, because he believed the Pope to be the Antichrist. In this conception he was followed by all his contemporaries. It was not given to the great reformers to be used in the revival of the prophetic Word and to give the midnight cry. Nor do we hear anything like the midnight cry immediately after the reformation; we go back to the first half of the last century and there we meet with a revival of the blessed Hope, the coming of the Lord. The Holy Spirit flashed forth this blessed truth once more and ever since then the midnight cry has been heard, and it is still being heard. We live in the fulfillment of this period of the parable of our Lord.

But what is indicated by these words? You noticed we left out the word "cometh." The authorized version reads, "Behold the Bridegroom cometh." The revised version has left out the word "cometh" and that is the right way to read it, "Behold the Bridegroom! Go ye forth to meet Him." This tells us that the midnight cry is more than a mere announcement of the coming of the Lord. It is, of course, indicated, but the Holy Spirit in the midnight cry calls attention to the person of the Bridegroom. He unfolds His glorious person anew and brings out the fact that His church, whom He has loved, is His Bride and that He is the Bridegroom. And along with this message of the Bridegroom there is a call to go forth to meet Him. What else is it than a call to the original position? It demands a return to that as it was in the beginning. It is a call to separation from all that is false and unscriptural. How can any one, or how could any one honestly believe that that adorable Person, the Bridegroom, is near, soon Coming, without turning away from all that is displeasing to Him, without turning the back upon all which dishonors both His Person and His Word? This then is the significant meaning of the midnight cry. Exactly this took place and still takes place in out present day. Along with the revival of the blessed Hope, the preaching of His imminent Coming, we have a return to other great truths, such as the teaching concerning the church. Just as the giving up of the blessed Hope affected the other great doctrines of the Bible and became in part responsible for the fearful decline, confusion and departure from the faith once and for all delivered unto the saints, so the recovery of the blessed Hope, the imminent Coming of the Lord, results in the recovery of these same blessed doctrines which were given up and leads to a return to the true position. All this has come to pass. All is still coming to pass. The midnight cry, "Behold the Bridegroom, go ye forth to meet Him," stands in closest connection with the church message to Philadelphia, in the third chapter of Revelation. There the *person* of Christ, as the Holy One and the True One, is in the foreground. Once more a company of His people at the very last days are keeping His Word and are not denying His name as well as keeping the Word of His patience, which has reference to His Coming, and to His Philadelphia remnant He gives the encouraging message, "I will keep thee out of the hour of trial which is to come upon all the earth." Philadelphia assuredly originates with the midnight cry. The two are inseparably connected.

But to return to the parable of the Lord. We notice that the midnight cry discovers the true condition of the wise and the foolish. They all arose and trimmed their lamps. The message has an effect upon the entire Christian profession. Of the wise we read but little, but the foolish now discover that they have no oil and further demonstrate their foolishness by appealing to the wise to give them oil. The wise in turn direct them to go to those who sell and buy for themselves. The words have occasioned much controversy.

It is not at all necessary that in a parable everything must have a definite meaning. It shows simply the utter blindness of these foolish one in looking to human beings for that which they lacked. The oil, the Holy Spirit, can be obtained only from Him, who gives without money and without price. But their foolishness just consisted in this very thing that they came not to Him, who is so willing to give. One can imagine the haste and activity of these foolish virgins in running here and there trying to get oil, to have burning lamps to meet the Bridegroom. It is exactly that which has happened since the midnight cry has been given and which we still witness about us. There is a great deal of religious activity, an immense amount of religious fervor, all kinds of endeavor and service, trying to do this and attempting to be better and do better. The so-called religious world feels that there is something in the air. Something is troubling them and yet they refuse to go to Him who alone can give and whose Grace alone can save and make ready. This is, alas, the sad condition of a great part of Christendom to-day. They hear the midnight cry and yet refuse to go to Him for oil.

But the wise arose and trimmed their lamps. They had the oil and they responded to the message, "Behold the Bridegroom! go ye forth to meet Him." It is a significant fact that the blessed Hope faithfully preached is causing separation between the true and the false. That is exactly why we must preach it and preach it more faithfully. And this continues. It has continued for a good many years, longer than those who were used by the Holy Spirit in the recovery of the blessed Hope, anticipated. The infinite patience of the Lord has delayed the next great event. How long will it all continue yet? Who can give us an answer to this? For all we know the next moment may usher in the actual appearing of the Bridegroom.

The next is "the Bridegroom came." How solemn this is. While the foolish kept on running and seeking and the wise had arisen and the separation between these classes had taken place, He came at last. *That is exactly what is before us now*. Oh! I wish I could impress it upon every heart that this solemn event may be upon us at any time. Surely the Bridegroom will not delay his coming much longer. When John the Baptist announced the first Coming of the King through the power and energy of the Holy Spirit did it take long for Him to come? And now for so many years already the Holy Spirit has announced the nearness of the Bridegroom, His soon Coming; can it then take much longer? Every waiting one, every spiritually minded believer who has intelligence, answers with thousands of others, "It cannot be much longer. He will tarry no more, but will quickly come."

How it fills our hearts with joy. The Bridegroom is coming and it reads, "They that were ready went in with him to the marriage." The wise, those who believe on the Lord Jesus Christ and know Him, are ready. Grace has made them ready and when He comes He will receive them. What a happy and glorious moment it will be at last. Said my little boy, who has an interest in the Coming of the Lord, "I wonder how He will look. I wonder what kind of a face He has when we see Him." That is exactly what you and I have often thought about and often wonder what it will be when we see Him at last as He is. And we *shall* see Him.

But there is another side, fearful indeed. "The door was shut." What words these are. The door closed in the face of the rest of the virgins. No more possibility, for them to enter in. Directly they come saying "Lord, Lord, open to us." But He answered and said, "Verily I say unto you, I know you not." They find themselves shut out. And let me say this is their final state. One of the fearful things with some of these new theories concerning this last parable is that they meddle with these last words addressed to the foolish virgins, as if they have another chance. No, no, the door was shut and when the door opens again He comes forth not as the Bridegroom, but as the King of kings and the Lord of lords, as the mighty judge. I know you not—what words from such lips! What eternal misery they foretell!

And this is the doom which hangs over the heads of the large masses of Christian people, Christians in name only, never saved. The moment He comes the door will be shut for these foolish virgins. Forever outside will be their destiny.

Perhaps I am speaking here to some, not many, but some, who have not the oil, who have not the Spirit of Christ and are none of His. Let me address these words to you, and if it is but one person. Delay no longer. Arise this very moment and go to Him who still waits in patience. He waits for you and invites you to come to Him to buy without money and without price. Oh! come now, confess yourself with all your religiousness perhaps and self-righteousness a lost sinner. You need to be no longer in that dangerous position. Believe on the Lord Jesus Christ; decide it now and I can assure you He will give you that which you lack in your empty profession; and should He come to-night, as may be the case, you will be ready to enter in with the oldest saint of God. He died for you to have you with Himself. Will you reject then the offer of salvation as it comes in this solemn hour? How can you? Delay no longer, but now cast yourself into His arms.

And we who know Him and wait for Him with longing hearts, there is more than one solemn message which comes to us from this parable. Think of the awful doom of the multitudes of professing, but unsaved, Christians. Some believers who believe in the eternal punishment of the unsaved act as if it were not true. If it is true as alas! it is, how can we be idle? Brethren, we have a great responsibility towards the foolish virgins, the great mass of the professing church. God forbid that we should be negligent in discharging this duty. Away with the miserable sectarian spirit which takes the skirts together, like the Pharisee of old and says, "I am holier than thou," and refuses to go to those who need the truth and the Gospel. We have a debt to pay; we are debtors to all. As long as the Bridegroom tarries let us go to those who are Christians in name and who know Him not and He will graciously own our testimony.

"Watch, therefore, for ye know not neither the day nor the hour." Soon all will be reality. Soon we shall enter in to be with the Bridegroom; shut in with Him. God grant that none of us may be shut out.

THE REDEMPTION OF THE PURCHASED POSSESSION
Ephes. i:13, 14; Rev. xii

We find in these words a truth revealed, which is quite often overlooked by readers of this great Epistle. It is this: The purchased possession, that which has been purchased for us, is yet to be redeemed. There is a future redemption of the purchased possession.

The divine statement includes this fact, that believers are sealed with the Holy Spirit of promise, and that He is the earnest or our inheritance until the time when the redemption of the purchased possession takes place.

And where do we find these words in this great chapter? If this chapter is at all to be divided, it must be divided into two parts. The first fourteen verses make the first part and then follows the great prayer of the Spirit of God through the Apostle. The statement which is before us for consideration is found at the end of the first part, preceding the prayer of the Apostle.

And what precious truth this chapter up to the fourteenth verse contains! It is indeed God's highest revelation concerning believing sinners saved by Grace. There is nothing higher than that, which is revealed here, and it is safe to say that God could not tell us anything better and more precious than what He has told us in this chapter.

First stands the greatest doxology of the Scriptures. "Blessed be the God and Father of our Lord Jesus Christ, who has blessed us with every spiritual blessing in the heavenlies in Christ." This takes it all together. We are as believers of Christ united to Him, One with Him and therefore we possess every spiritual blessing the God and Father of our Lord Jesus Christ is capable of giving. Then follows the great facts connected with our redemption in Christ. Here we find election, predestination, adoption, or putting into the Son-place, Redemption, the source of redemption as well as the prize of redemption.

Let us glance briefly at those glorious steps which lead up to our verse. They are just seven.

We can only name them, much as we would like to ponder over each. 1. We are chosen in Him before the foundation of the world. He thought of us and loved us before ever a single thing had been created. 2. Marked out for the Son-place through Jesus Christ. According to the good pleasure of His will He has given us the place of a Son. 3. He has taken us into the favor in the Beloved. In that beloved One we are beloved forever accepted in Him. 4. We have redemption through His blood, the

51

forgiveness of offences, according to the riches of His grace. 5. Then we have the knowledge of the mystery of His will, according to His good pleasure which He purposed in Himself for the administration of the fulness of times, to head up all things in the Christ. 6. In Him we have obtained an inheritance; and then the last step, the seventh, we are sealed with the Holy Spirit of promise, the earnest of that inheritance which we have obtained.

Now let me just say this little word on the last great fact. The authorized version reads "after that ye believed ye were sealed with that holy Spirit of promise." This translation is misleading and gives ground to an error which is becoming more and more widespread. It is the error that the Holy Spirit is not given at once when the sinner believes, but that the Holy Spirit is received in a definite experience after we have believed. It is an error; the passage before us does not teach this but the very opposite, for it reads, "in whom also believing, ye were sealed with the Holy Spirit." Every one who has believed received in the act of believing the Holy Spirit. And this blessed gift, not an influence, but the person of the Holy Spirit, is both the seal and the earnest. A seal makes secure and denotes safety. By that seal we are owned by God. We are His property, we belong to Him. Then the Holy Spirit is the earnest of our inheritance, the pledge of it. We give an earnest when we buy a property, it is an advance payment, the first installment. So is the Holy Spirit from the side of our God the earnest of the purchased possession. How happy and full of joy we should be with the knowledge of all these precious truths, with the seal and earnest of our possession.

But the earnest (not the seal) is up to a certain time and that time is when we come into the full possession of our inheritance "until the redemption of the purchased possession to the praise of His glory." This brings us to the whole matter before us.

1. In the first place what is "our inheritance" mentioned here? We find the word inheritance three times in this chapter. "In whom we have also obtained an inheritance" (verse 11). Then in the 14th verse, "The earnest of our inheritance." We find it again in the 18th verse. "So that ye should know what is the hope of His calling and what the riches of the glory of His inheritance in the Saints." The inheritance is, according to these passages, twofold. Believers constituting the church have an inheritance and we are His inheritance. The inheritance we have, our inheritance, is nothing less than the inheritance of the Christ. He made Him Heir of all things. He is the Heir of God. The same is said of us as believers. We are heirs of God and joint heirs with the Lord Jesus Christ. God has put us, according to the good pleasure of His will in Christ, in the place of sons and because He has made us sons He has made us heirs. The inheritance

52

of the first begotten from the dead is the inheritance of all who are by Grace constituted sons in Him. And what is His inheritance which we shall share in all eternity? We find in it the preceding verses, "having made known unto us the mystery of His will, according to His good pleasure which He purposed in Himself for the administration of the fulness of times; to head up all things in the Christ, the things in the heavens and the things upon the earth." In other words, He is the heir of all things and these include both the heavens and the earth. All is put under His feet. And this glorious inheritance belongs to us; we shall share it with Him in all eternity. What mind and heart can grasp it! It is unspeakable and unfathomable. Our inheritance is often lowered in that people speak about the earth as being the inheritance. Certain passages from the Old Testament are quoted in support of this. "The meek shall inherit the earth," "the earth has He given to the children of men." But this does not at all refer to our inheritance, but rather to the inheritance of an earthly people in the millennium. Our inheritance assuredly includes the earth, but the heavens are the supreme place for the church. As He is now far above all principalities and power and might and dominion, in the heavenlies, so will the church occupy the heavenlies with Him, the glorified Head, and in the ages to come God will show in this very position and possession He has given to us His exceeding riches of His Grace.

But here we read not only of an inheritance, which belongs to us, but it speaks of "the purchased possession." There is no difference at all between these two terms "our inheritance" and "the purchased possession;" they are one and the same thing. The inheritance, the possession of the heavenlies and of the earth is acquired or purchased and the purchase price is the blood of the Son of God. The precious blood of the Son of God has not only redeemed us and made it possible for us to share His inheritance to the praise of His Glory, but it has also purchased both the heavenlies and the earth. The heavenlies as well as the things on earth have been defiled by sin and needed the purchase; the blood of the Son of God alone could accomplish that. In the same sense we read in the first chapter of Colossians of the reconciliation of all things, the things in heaven and the things on the earth.

It is an interesting fact that we find the same word "the purchased possession" as it is translated here at four other places in the New Testament. Twice in Thessalonians, once in Hebrews and once in 1st Peter. Each time it refers to the future.

1 Thess. v:9. "God has not set us for wrath, but (literally) unto acquiring salvation through our Lord Jesus Christ, who has died for us that whether we may be watching or sleep, we may live together with

Him. The "acquiring of salvation" is future and corresponds to the "purchased possession."

2 Thess. ii:14. "Unto which He called you through our Gospel, unto an acquiring of the Glory of the Lord Jesus Christ."

1 Peter ii:19.... "A people for an acquisition;" that is, a people formed for a possession corresponding to Isaiah xliii:2. "This people have I formed for myself, they shall show forth my praise." This is spoken, of course, concerning Israel. It also finds an application in the church, the royal Priesthood. In the possession of our inheritance we shall make known His excellencies, His Glory.

Hebrews x:39. The word is likewise found also relating to the future, "the preservation of the soul," the same as salvation in the future sense.

2. And now we reach the main thought of the Scripture before us. The purchased possession, the inheritance, though it has been fully paid for, is completely purchased, is yet to be redeemed. While we said that our inheritance and the expression "the purchased possession" are the same, it is not so with "purchase" and "redemption." These are two different things. The purchase is by blood, but the redemption here is by power. The purchased possession is to be redeemed by power.

Now as this is so the inheritance must be in a state of alienation from God; some power has hold of it who has no right to it. If this were not the case it would be impossible to speak of a redemption by power. It is just like the possession of some land in a frontier state. A person purchases a large tract of land. It is his, he has a perfect title to it. But now he comes and looks over his purchased possession and he finds a number of people who settled upon it. They have erected houses and make a claim that it belongs to them, but they have no right to it at all. Either by law or by force they are to be evicted from the property to which they have no right. At a certain time the owner comes and claims his ownership and casts out these people. And even so that which the Lord has purchased and which belongs to Him and to the sons of God with Him, His inheritance and our inheritance is possessed up to this time by evil, God opposing powers and they have still control of it till the hour of eviction comes. All things are indeed put under His feet, but we see not yet all things put under Him, though we see as a pledge that it shall be so, "Jesus who was made a little lower than the angels for the suffering of death crowned with glory and honor." The earth is the Lord's and the fullness thereof, and yet the earth is still in the grasp of that mighty being, who had shown to our Lord the kingdoms of this world claiming them as his own and offering the same to the Lord. The father of lies spoke the truth then, for the kingdoms of this world are in his possession and they are still his. He is still the god of this age, the prince of the world. The enemies of Christ seen and unseen are not yet made His footstool, nor will they be till the power of God does it in that mighty act of a future redemption. Still there is the groaning of all creation, waiting for something better to come, waiting for the deliverance from the bondage of corruption, waiting to be brought into the glorious liberty of the children of God. The deliverance of groaning creation takes place when the sons of God are manifested, and that is the time of the redemption of the purchased possession. And we also who have the first fruits of the Spirit, groan within ourselves, waiting for the adoption, the redemption of the body. And the redemption of the body belongs to the redemption of the purchased possession.

And how is it with the heavens? Surely here we cannot speak of some evil powers holding possessions, and that it is necessary to redeem that possession by power? It is exactly this which is mostly before us in this epistle of the Heavenlies.

To some Christians this is almost impossible to grasp and yet it is clearly revealed in the Scriptures that the heavenlies, the sphere above the earth and way beyond, is in the grasp of the evil tenants which under the headship of Satan form mighty principalities and powers and dominions. He himself as head reaches into heaven and has access to the very throne itself. He is not only the god of this age and the prince of this world, but also "The prince of the power in the air." How mighty he is as such, what powers are at his disposal, how vast his kingdom is, how numerous the fallen beings with him and how the demons fill the air, no saint has ever fully realized, nor shall we ever realize it, till the God of peace has Satan completely bruised under our feet.

Think for a moment of what the Scriptures say. There is the first and second chapter in the Book of Job. Some call it fiction. We call it one of the greatest revelations of the Word of God. There is the throne of God, and to that throne comes Satan as the accuser of the brethren. The New Testament verifies that this is still the case, and that at the present time this mighty being still accuses the saints of God before the throne of righteousness. And that is one of the reasons why the Lord Jesus Christ as our advocate appears in the presence of God for us.

Again we read the words of a prophet. "I saw the Lord sitting on His throne and all the host of heaven standing by him on his right and on his left.... And there came forth a spirit and stood before the Lord and said, I will persuade him (King Ahab). And the Lord said unto him, Wherewith? And he said, I will go forth and I will be a lying spirit in the mouth of all his prophets" (1 Kings xxii:19-23). And furthermore here in the Epistle to Ephesians in the last chapter we read of the warfare of the

Christian believer, which is not with flesh and blood but against principalities, against powers, against the rulers of the darkness of this world, against the wicked spirits in the heavenlies. This passage alone is sufficient evidence to show that the heavenlies are up to the present time tenanted by wicked spirits. They hold possession of the heavenlies and have control there. But Christ has triumphed over Satan and his wicked spirits and has purchased that heavenly possession. It belongs to Him and to His church, and when the right time comes the redemption of that possession will take place and the heavenlies will be cleared from these usurpers.

3. This brings us to the third thought connected with this theme. *When and how will the purchased possession be redeemed by the power of God?* We are not left to speculation on this matter, for while we have here just a few words concerning this great event we have in another part of the Bible a revelation, which may be termed the complete history of the redemption of the purchased possession. There we have the when and the how we have asked completely answered. That book is our great New Testament Book of Prophecy, the Revelation. The parts in which the redemption of the purchased possession by the power of God is revealed are chapters xii and xx.

The twelfth chapter is one of the great chapters in this marvelous book. It is not only a great chapter, but also an important one. In examining any exposition of the Book of Revelation one does well to turn to this chapter and read what the expositor has to say on it. If he is straight here his book is well worth reading; if not he must be wrong in the greater part of the book. The great vision is the woman travailing in pain to be delivered of a manchild. The catching away of that manchild, which the red dragon was ready to devour. The casting out of Satan after the manchild is with God and in heaven, the persecution of the woman and her seed by the serpent. The erroneous interpretation always concerns the woman. Many make her to be the church, and then the manchild is a select company of the elect church, overcomers, first fruits, or as some call them the 144,000.

The woman has nothing to do with the church. She typifies Israel and this is easily verified from Old Testament passages. The manchild destined to rule the nations with a rod of iron is Christ who, according to the flesh, came from Israel. Satan hated Him and would have devoured Him, but could not. The man-child is caught away and then after He is in the presence of God all the other events come rapidly to pass.

We notice that a number of important things are passed over entirely in the beginning of this chapter. They are implied, of course. Nothing is said of the earthly life of Christ, nothing of His death and resurrection.

They are implied in His being caught away unto God. There is nothing said of this present age and nothing of the church, but she is likewise implied in this scene. The manchild does not stand for the person of Christ alone, but for the completed Christ, I mean by this the Christ, the Head and the Body, the church united to Him in Glory. What is spoken of the Christ in resurrection is also spoken of His church. The promise to rule the nations with a rod of iron is not only to Him but through Him also to those who overcome. "And he shall rule them with a rod of iron, as the vessels of a potter shall they be broken to shivers, even as I received of my Father" (Rev. ii:28). It is also significant that we do not read of the ascension here of our Lord. If the word were here that the man-child ascended, I doubt if then we could say the church is implied, for the word ascension is never used in connection with the church. But it reads "Caught away," and the very same word which is used here is used in 1 Thess. iv. "Caught up together with them in clouds." What follows next is the war in heaven and the casting out of Satan. This will not take place till the complete church, the Body and Bride of Christ, is taken up. Then Satan will be completely bruised under our feet. In spite of his malice, in spite of his power and accusations, in spite of his challenge to God and fearful attacks, there is not one member of that glorious body missing, all the redeemed are in the presence of the Lord and then Satan is forced down to the earth by Michael and his angels. In heaven there is a loud voice which declares: "Now is come salvation and strength, and the kingdom of our God, and the power of His Christ, for the accuser of our brethren is cast down, which accused them day and night before our God. And they overcame him by the blood of the Lamb, and by the word of their testimony, and they loved not their lives unto death. Therefore rejoice, oh ye heavens, and ye that dwell in them." Then Satan as the accuser has no more place in heaven and the advocacy of Christ concerning His own, as He said in His highpriestly prayer, "I pray for them," has an end. They are all safe with Him in glory.

The heavenlies are thus cleared of Satan and his hosts when the church is brought in and the eviction is the redemption of the purchased possession. It takes place by the power of God through the mighty Being whose name is "Who is like God," Michael.

Satan the usurper cast out of the heavenly sphere goes down to the earth having great wrath. How fearful must be the wrath of that Being! Who of us can imagine it, what it will be? Surely the Lord would never leave His church, His Bride on the earth, when that awful Being with that great wrath comes down. Indeed what we have said shows clearly that the great tribulation is impossible as long as the church, the complete church, is not yet in glory. For to have the great tribulation on the earth the old serpent must be cast down on the earth.

The redemption of the purchased possession begins then with the rapture of the church to be with Christ in His Inheritance in the Heavenlies. This is followed by Satan being cast out of heaven. And then a few years more and the heavens open and the King of kings and Lord of lords appears. The Son in all His Glory is manifested bringing many sons with Him to Glory. It is then that we have the redemption of the purchased possession completed. "And I saw an angel come down from heaven, having the key of the bottomless pit and a great chain in his hand. And he laid hold on the dragon, that old Serpent, which is the Devil and Satan, and bound him a thousand years and cast him into the bottomless pit, and shut him up, and set a seal upon him, that he should deceive the nations no more, till the thousand years should be fulfilled, and after that he must be loosed a little season. And I saw thrones and they sat upon them, and the judgment was given unto them, and I saw the souls of them that were beheaded for the witness of Jesus, and for the Word of God, and which had not worshipped the beast, neither his image, neither had received his mark upon their foreheads, or in their hands; and they lived and reigned with Christ a thousand years" (Rev. xx:1-5).

Then all of groaning creation will be delivered and Satan will no longer be the god of this age, the prince of this world nor the prince of the power in the air. There will be peace on earth and Glory to God in the Highest. Christ will reign and His church with Him in the Glory above. What a time it will be when it comes. What singing in heaven and on the earth. Then shall He have His full inheritance which we share and also have His inheritance in us His Saints, and He will be admired in all them that have believed. And all this is near.

Just a little while longer and we shall hear His shout which calls us and all His redeemed into His presence, with bodies redeemed by His power to enter into our inheritance, the purchased possession.

And now two things need to be mentioned in closing. Our conflict is with these evil spirits, the usurpers, both in the heavenlies and here on earth. May we be victors through the power of the Christ in us and His Spirit. The conflict is becoming hotter, especially for those who enter into their privileges and realize in faith their place and future glory.

Let us also walk worthy of our calling. Let it be seen that we are sealed by the Holy Spirit and have Him as the earnest of our inheritance. A Christian who professes to have such an inheritance and who professes to wait for the redemption of the purchased possession and who grasps after the honors of the world and runs after its riches is a sad spectacle indeed.

THE HISTORY OF SATAN

Satan is a person and has a history. No intelligent believer in the Bible denies this, for the Bible teaches in both Testaments that such a being exists, and more than that, the history of this person is given in the Word of God. He is not a divine being, but a creature. His origin, his work and his final destiny are revealed in the Scriptures. Yet it needs to be stated that much in connection with this person is obscure and that certain facts can only be learned by inference. Questions are often asked concerning this being, which no one can answer. We mean these questions "Why God created such a being, if He knew that he would be His enemy and do the awful work he has done and which he is still doing," or "Why does God still permit him to do this work and why does He not end his career?" In such matters it behooves us to confess our ignorance and also our faith in an all-wise God, whose wisdom, sovereignty and justice are perfect. Some day these unrevealed mysteries will be all cleared up for the Saints of God.

What Person He Was

The conception, which originated in the middle ages, in connection with the gross perversion of the truth of God, that this person is one of repulsive and grotesque countenance, with the figure of a monstrosity, is an invention and cannot be verified from Scripture. The Bible knows nothing of such a being with a horrible face and figure. The very opposite is the teaching of the Word of God. He was originally the greatest and most marvelous creation of God. Though now fallen and the enemy of God, he still retains much of his original beauty and wisdom. In Isaiah xiv:12 the word "Lucifer" (lightbearer) refers to him. He is called "Son of the Morning." That must have been his name when unfallen. Still more striking is the description of the same person in one of the great prophetic utterances of Ezekiel. In chapter xxviii:11-19 we read the following:

"Moreover the word of the Lord came unto me, saying, Son of man, take up a lamentation upon the king of Tyrus, and say unto him, Thus saith the Lord God; Thou sealest up the sum, full of wisdom, and perfect in beauty. Thou hast been in Eden, the garden of God; every precious stone was thy covering, the sardius, topaz, and the diamond, the beryl, the onyx, and the jasper, the sapphire, the emerald, and the carbuncle, and gold: the workmanship of thy tabrets and of thy pipes was prepared in thee in the day that thou wast created. Thou art the anointed cherub that covereth; and I have set thee so; thou was upon the holy mountain of God; thou hast walked up and down in the midst of the stones of fire. Thou wast perfect in thy ways from the day that thou was created, till iniquity was found in thee. By the multitude of thy merchandise they have filled the midst of thee with violence, and thou hast sinned: therefore I will cast thee as profane out of the mountain of God: and I will destroy thee, O covering cherub, from the midst of the stones of fire. Thine heart was lifted up because of thy beauty, thou hast corrupted thy wisdom by reason of thy brightness: I will cast thee to the ground, I will lay thee before kings, that they may behold thee."

These words are words of lamentation over the wicked king of Tyrus. While this king is mentioned the description does not fit him at all, but must be applied to the one who was the unseen power behind the throne of the Tyrian king. The great city of Tyrus, once so glorious and now forever gone, is a type of the commercial glory of the world, its wealth and its prince, foreshadowing the final great world-city and world-system Babylon. Satan controlled Tyrus as he will also control the coming, final Babylon. We have therefore here a description of Satan in his original condition as an unfallen creature. He was full of wisdom and perfect in beauty. He was in Eden the garden of God and every precious stone was his covering. He was the anointed cherub that covereth, perhaps an archangel like Michael. He was in the mountain of God and perfect in the day of his creation.

We quote another passage from which we may learn by inference his original greatness and majesty. Jude predicts the final apostasy of this present age, which culminates in man despising dominions and speaking evil of dignities. He then makes a statement in which Satan is mentioned: "Yet Michael the archangel, when contending with the devil he disputed about the body of Moses, durst not bring against him a railing accusation, but said, the Lord rebuke thee" (verses 8-9). It is a unique revelation nowhere else found in the Bible that when Moses' body was to be laid away, the devil appeared on the scene. Perhaps Michael was commissioned by the Lord to bury the body of Moses. The devil evidently laid claim to the body of God's servant. Perhaps he wanted the body to be preserved in an embalmed condition as an object of idolatry. When Michael faced him he durst not bring a railing accusation against him. He still recognized in him, though fallen, the greatness of his original being. This is sufficient to show that Satan was once a mighty, glorious, majestic being, full of wisdom and beauty. Being a creature he is not omnipotent, nor is he omniscient or omnipresent.

His Fall

His fall and how he became the great enemy of God is also revealed. We find it in the two chapters already quoted, Isaiah xiv and Ezekiel xxviii. He said in his heart "I will ascend into heaven, I will exalt my throne above the stars of God; I will sit also upon the mount of the congregation in the sides of the north. I will ascend above the heights of the clouds, I will be like the Most High" (Isaiah xiv:13-14). Ezekiel's prophecy tells us that iniquity was found in him. "Thine heart was lifted up because of thy beauty, thou has corrupted thy wisdom by reason of thy brightness" (Ezek. xxviii:17). In the beginning of this chapter a similar statement is made, which also must be applied to Satan. "Thus saith the Lord God, because thine heart is lifted up, and thou hast said, I am a God and sit in the seat of God." The New Testament also bears witness to the fact and reminds us of the above revelations in 1 Timothy iii:6. Speaking of the qualifications of an elder, we read, "Not a novice, lest being lifted up with pride he fall into the condemnation of the devil." The word condemnation has the meaning of "crime" in the Greek. He revolted against God; he was not satisfied with the position and place the Creator had given him and aimed to occupy the throne above the stars and be like the Most High. Then he fell and became the enemy of God, which he still is and ever will be. In his attempt to become like the Most High other angels sided with him and shared in the fall likewise.

Where Was His Original Dwelling Place

If this being attempted to put his throne above the stars, then must he have had a throne somewhere else. If he aimed to ascend into heaven and be like the Most High, he must have had some dwelling place which God had assigned to him. There is no positive Scripture concerning this place. Yet by inferential evidence the knowledge can be gained that our earth in its original condition was the domain of this great creature of God.

"In the beginning God created the heavens and the earth." We do not know when this was. In certain Bible editions the date 4004 B. C. is placed in the margin over against Gen. i:1. But that is incorrect. It would make the earth not quite 6000 years old. Science has demonstrated the fact that our globe is of a very great age. No human being can tell the exact time when God created the heavens and the earth. It may have been 2 million or 20 million or 200 million years ago. We know, however, that the human race became a recent tenant on this earth. The human race is not older than about 6000 years.

In that distant past before man was created the earth was in a different form. At that time there was a gigantic animal creation and an equally gigantic vegetation in existence. It has been brought to light through the fossil beds; but in none of these fossils is found a trace of a human being. This great original creation was plunged at one time into an awful catastrophe. Death and destruction came upon it, every living thing was extinguished, while water covered everything and all was enveloped in darkness.

This is exactly the condition of the earth as described in the second verse of the Bible. "And the earth was without form and void; and darkness was upon the face of the deep." If we turn to Isaiah xlv:18 we find a significant statement: "For thus saith the Lord who created the heavens; God himself that formed the earth and made it; He hath established it, He created it not in vain; He formed it to be inhabited." The word vain (tohu) is the same word used in Gen. i:2 and translated "without form." From this we learn that God did not originally create the earth as without form and void, enshrouded in darkness. It became this through a judgment which fell upon it. Between the first and second verses of the first chapter of Genesis is therefore a long, immeasurable period of time. Now, if this original earth was ruined and passed through a judgment, why did this ruin and judgment take place? This question must remain unanswered unless we bring that first judgment in connection with the revolt and fall of Satan, who had his dwelling place on this earth. This explains not only the ruined condition of the earth in Gen. i:2, but throws a great deal of light on Satan's successful attempt to get back his lost dominion through man and his tenacious hold on the earth, as the prince of the world and god of this age.[1]

Man Upon The Earth

In God's own time this earth was put into the condition to become the habitation for the human race. Of this we read in Genesis i:3-31. God then created man in His own image, and said, "Let them have dominion over the fish of the sea, and over the fowl of the air, and over the cattle, and over all the earth, and over every creeping thing that creepeth upon the earth" (Gen. i:26). "And God blessed them, and God said unto them, Be fruitful, and multiply, and replenish the earth, and subdue it, and have dominion over the fish of the sea, and over the fowl of the air, and over everything that moveth upon the earth." Thus the earth, which was originally Satan's habitation, was given to man.

The Fall of Man

When all this took place this great fallen being was no doubt an eyewitness. He beheld God working in rearranging the chaos of the original earth produced by his revolt. He saw how God created man. He heard how God spoke to man and gave him to possess his former estate which he had lost by his rebellion. He beheld God putting man and woman into the garden of Eden. He listened when God said "Of the tree of knowledge of good and evil thou shalt not eat of it, for in the day that thou eatest thereof thou shalt surely die" (Gen. ii:17). Then he must have been moved with envy and jealousy. He sees another in possession of his past domain. Something like this must have come into his mind—if I only can get man ruined and turn him against God, if I can make of man a rebel and lay hold on him, I shall get back the place which once was mine and then defy God.

The third chapter in Genesis shows how he succeeded in carrying out this plan. Through the serpent he approached the woman and said, "Yea, hath God said, Ye shall not eat of any tree of the garden?" God had spoken; the first word to man had come from His lips. Satan's first work was to make God's creature doubt God's Word. The first destructive critic who denied that God hath spoken was Satan. Every man, no matter what learning he may claim, who denies the inspiration of the Bible, and that the Bible is the revelation and Word of God, is the mouthpiece of Satan. Emboldened by the woman's answer he said "Ye shall not surely die," an out and out denial of what God had said; and then adds the lying promise, "Your eyes shall be opened and ye shall be as gods." He wanted to be like the Most High, and now he injects his own character into man. The transgression followed; sin came into the world and death by sin, the moment God's commandment was disobeyed. What a sneer and laughter, what a triumphant shout Satan must have uttered when the deed was done! And with the fall of man he laid hold again on this earth and became its prince.

Satan's Doom Announced

Then the Lord sought that which was lost, the guilty pair, and addressed the serpent. The words the Lord then spoke contain the first prophecy of the Bible. It concerns Satan, how God will deal with him and his final doom. "And I will put enmity between thee and the woman, and between thy seed and her seed; it shall bruise thy head and thou shalt bruise his heel" (Gen. iii:15). Without fully explaining this prophecy, which may well be termed the germ of all subsequent prophecy, we but point out what it means. From the woman there is to come a seed, an offspring who is to bruise the head of the serpent (Satan), that is, overcome the serpent, and that the serpent is to bruise the heel of the seed of the woman. Furthermore, there is to rage a conflict between the serpent and the woman and between the serpent's seed and the seed of the woman. There can be no question whatever that the seed of the woman means the Son of God in His incarnation. Paul writes to the Galatians, "But when the fulness of time was come God sent forth His Son made of a woman" (Gal. iv:4). He is the seed of the woman, the virgin-born Son of God. His death is mentioned in this first prophecy as the bruising of His heel. Then the final victory over Satan and his final doom, his head is to be bruised. And till that is accomplished there is to be conflict between the seed of the woman and the seed of the serpent, a conflict between those who side with God, believe on and wait for the promised One, and those who side with Satan and his works. Satan heard then from the lips of Jehovah that the seed of the woman would conquer him and seal his doom.

His Work and the Conflict Begins

The predicted conflict began at once. Two sons are born to Adam and Eve. Satan watched them. He is interested to see if one of them might be "the seed." He saw Cain bringing an offering of the fruit of the ground (the labor of his hands) unto the Lord.[2] Satan must have been delighted with Cain, as he beheld him, as a self-righteous man, rejecting God's provision for him as a sinner. He knew Cain was his man and belonged to his seed. It was different with Abel. Abel brought of the firstlings of the flock and of the fat thereof. "By faith Abel offered unto God a more excellent sacrifice than Cain, by which he obtained witness that he was righteous, God testifying of his gifts" (Heb. xi:3). He was a believer, who owned himself as a sinner and because he believed, God accepted his offering. As Satan beheld this scene he must have imagined that Abel was "the seed of the woman." Then he filled Cain with wrath and moved him to slay his brother Abel. Thus Satan manifested himself in the beginning of the human race as the liar and the murderer. Our Lord testified of this character of the enemy when He spoke to those who conspired to kill Him and who belonged to the Devil's seed: "Ye are of your father the devil, and the lusts of your father ye will do. He was a murderer from the beginning, and abode not in the truth, because there is no truth in him. When he speaketh a lie, he speaketh of his own; for he is a liar and the father of it" (John viii:44). But the murder of Abel was unavailing. Eve bore another son "and called his name Seth, for God,

64

said she, hath appointed me another seed instead of Abel, whom Cain slew" (Gen. iv:25). Satan was defeated for the first time.

An Interesting History

An interesting history follows. The Old Testament history is the history of conflict between the seed of the serpent and the seed of the woman. Satan continually worked to oppose God, attempting to prevent the coming of that promised seed of the woman. He knew if he succeeded in this he would not again be dispossessed from this planet and his own doom would never come. Besides trying to prevent the coming of the promised One, his aim is to control the nations, have dominion over them, and to deny the truth of God made known to man by revelation. He corrupted the human race before the deluge so that the earth was corrupt before God and filled with violence (Gen. vi:11). This great being knew well that God is holy and cannot tolerate evil. He plunged the race into great wickedness in the hope that God would destroy the whole race and leave him possessor of the earth. But Noah found grace in the sight of the Lord.

When Satan received the knowledge that the seed to conquer him and seal his doom would come through Abraham, he then opposed the seed of Abraham to frustrate God's purpose. The land which was promised by Jehovah to Abraham and his descendants was settled by the nations which were Satan-controlled and were his willing instruments. Satan's power in wickedness and vileness was manifested in the Canaanites. That is why the Lord commanded their utter extermination. So that in the land itself there was a steady conflict between the seed of the serpent, the Canaanites, and the seed of the woman, godly Israelites.

When Pharaoh gave the command to kill all the male children born to Israel in Egypt, it was another attempt of Satan to make the coming of the promised seed impossible (Ex. i:16). But God took care and used the Hebrew midwives, the weaker vessels, to bring to naught the wicked plan. Pharaoh brought up in his own palace one of the Hebrew boys, whom Satan would have killed; and that boy became the great leader and deliverer of Israel. All the persecutions of the people Israel in Egypt were Satan's work. When at last they had left the house of bondage, Satan in impotent rage stirred up Pharaoh to attempt their destruction; but Pharaoh and his army found their graves in the Red Sea.

Afterward Jehovah announced that the promised seed should be of the house of David. Then Satan watched David and his descendants. Through Saul he persecuted God's anointed, but failed to touch his life. Immediately after the Lord had made the covenant with David (2 Sam.

vii) promising him a son whose Kingdom shall be established (the seed—Christ), Satan led David to commit his awful sin. Jehoram, the son of Jehoshaphat, belonged to the seed of the serpent. This wicked son of David slew all his brethren. It was Satan's attempt to exterminate the descendant of David (2 Chronicles xxi:4). Then the Arabians came and slew all his sons except Ahaziah. Still greater was Satan's attempt to end forever the house of David through wicked queen Attaliah. She was the mother of Ahaziah. When her son had been slain "she arose and destroyed all the seed royal of the house of Judah" (2 Chronicles xxii:10). Satan had made the awful suggestion to her and when the seed royal was destroyed he thought he had triumphed at last. "But Jehoshabeath, the daughter of the King, took Joash the son of Ahaziah, and stole him from the King's sons that were slain, and put him and his nurse in a bedchamber. So Jehoshabeath, the daughter of King Jehoram, the wife of Jehorada the priest, hid him from Attaliah so that she slew him not. And he was with them hid in the house of God six years" (2 Chron. xxvii:11-12). Satan was defeated.

Through Haman he made still another attempt to have all the Jews, men, women, and children, killed. God watched over His people again and Satan's plan was frustrated. And how much else might be added! Throughout Old Testament history he had his chosen instruments, like Nimrod, the kings of Babylon, the Pharaohs, the Assyrian, the Persian Kings, Alexander and others through whom he attempted world dominion. He instigated the cruel and terrible wars. Israel, the people of God, were led by him into idolatry and apostasy. In all this and much besides his aim was the defiance of God and to keep God from carrying out his plan of redemption though the promised seed.

The Promised Seed and Satan's Opposition

The promised seed came. The Son of God took on the creature's garb and became man, the son of David and son of Abraham, according to the flesh. All Satan had done for 4,000 years had been in vain. God had kept His promise. King Herod was the seed of the serpent and when the child was born, Satan moved him to seek the young child to destroy him. Herod, inspired by the murderer from the beginning, "exceeding wroth, sent forth and slew all the children that were in Bethlehem, and in all the coasts thereof from two years old and under" (Matt. ii:16). But God had watched, and the young child was on the way to Egypt when Satan's suggestion was carried out by the Roman soldiers.

And how many more times he must have made the same attempt! When Satan had taken him on the pinnacle of the temple and suggested "cast thyself down," he tried it once more. The people of Nazareth were the serpent's seed and under his control when they rushed him out of the city and attempted to cast him headlong down a precipice. The storms on the lake were Satan's work to take His life. Little did he know that the ship in which the Son of God slept peacefully, though it filled with water, was the only unsinkable ship which sailed the seas. He could not touch the seed of the woman, for He was holy, without sin, and death had not claim on Him.

Yet He had come to die "that through death He might destroy him that had the power of death, that is, the devil." He knew that the Lord Jesus would get the victory and the dominion over this earth by the way of the Cross. That is why he took Him on the exceeding high mountain and showed him all the kingdoms of the world, and the glory of them. He offered all to the Son of Man, if He but would fall down before him. He wanted Him to keep away from the cross for he knew then and knows now, far better than many a so-called theologian, that redemption for the individual and redemption for this earth, the nations and groaning creation has its blessed source in the work of the Cross. He was defeated in all his malice and cunning. And finally the Cross, preceded by the agony in Gethsemane. Satan was there; with unspeakable hatred he planned His death. He entered into Judas; he used the Pharisees and Sadducees, the priests and elders, which were all Satan's seed, to have Him put to death. The cry "Away with Him! Crucify Him!" was inspired by himself. He used man to dishonor the Son of God, to revile Him, spit in His face, to scourge Him and finally to nail Him to the Cross. Did he think that he might yet get the victory and keep the Lord Jesus from finishing the work the Father gave Him to do? We do not know if such was the case, but we know that while the Son of God gave Himself, Satan had also his part in His rejection and His death. Our Lord conquered. He won the victory and those blessed never-to-be-forgotten words, "It is finished" tell of the final doom of Satan and the coming glories of a new heaven and a new earth. The thorn-crowned Man of that cross of shame will some day be the glory-crowned Man who claims His inheritance, and because he wore the thorns and paid for all sin's curse, He will rid this earth from the works of the devil.

The tomb was closed with the big stone and then sealed with the Roman seal. A watch too is set. How careful Satan is! What a good memory he has! Yet how blind! He wanted to prevent His triumphant resurrection, as if he had more power than God! On the third day the stone was rolled away. He came forth. Death and the grave are conquered. He is the resurrection and the life. Then the man-child, whom the dragon wanted to devour (Rev. xii) was caught up to the throne of

God, destined to rule the nations with a rod of iron. Like another Joash, He is hidden in the house of God. He fills the throne there and awaits in that place of glorious exaltation the time when Satan will be dethroned and He, the Son of Man, will receive His own throne.

The Conflict Continues

As stated elsewhere, Satan by having succeeded in getting the Jews and Gentiles to reject the Prince of Life and the Lord of Glory, became what he has not been in previous ages, "the god of this age" (2 Cor. iv:4).[3] And so the conflict continues. Satan can no longer attempt to prevent the coming of the promised seed or attack His Person, for He is in glory as the glorified Man. He knows, however, that He has a seed on this earth, a seed which has the promise given that he, Satan, "is to be bruised completely" under their feet. This seed is the church. The enmity and conflict during this present age is therefore between the seed of the serpent and the seed of Christ, those who are in Him and in whom Christ dwelleth.

All students of Prophecy know that the seven church messages in the book of Revelation (chapters ii and iii) contain a prophetic forecast of the history of the church on earth, from the apostolic age to the time when the true church is taken to glory and the apostate church disowned by the Lord.[4] In these prophetic messages Satan's work in opposition to the church is made known. In the Apostolic age he acted in introducing error; he sowed the tares. After the Apostles had passed away a time of great persecution set in which is indicated in the message to Smyrna. The Roman emperors were the serpent's seed. They claimed divine honors and worship. As Satan's instruments they persecuted the church, and thousands upon thousands of believers died the martyrs' death. The cruel tortures and horrible forms of death were Satan's work by which he attempted to exterminate the church. When he found that the blood of the martyrs was the seed of the church, and that the church increased in spite of these persecutions, then he began to corrupt the church. The professing church settled down where Satan's throne is, that is, she gave up the place of separation and became a world institution. Gradually the Gospel and the doctrine of Christ became perverted, heathenish customs were introduced and finally the culmination was reached in the Romish apostasy. These developments are described in the messages to Pergamos and Thyatira. When the Reformation set in the fires of persecution were kindled again; once more Satan, as the murderer, tries to prevent the victory of the truth of Christ and the Gospel. Satan's work can thus be traced in the history of the church down to our own times. The destructive criticism of our own times, the so-called "new theology," the different systems, which deny the Deity of our Lord and which reject His atoning death, like "Christian Science," belong to the seed of the serpent. And so does Spiritism, Theosophy, Mormonism and other cults. In these systems and cults he appears as an angel of light, blinding the eyes of them that believe not. "And no marvel, for Satan himself is transformed into an angel of light, therefore it is no great thing if his ministers also be transformed as the ministers of righteousness, whose end shall be according to their works" (2 Cor. xi:14-15).

Why He Hates the Church

He hates the true church because he knows its members are the blood-bought hosts of the Son of God, destined to rule and reign with Him over this earth, which Satan still holds in his grasp. There is another reason why he has tried to exterminate the true church or to corrupt it. Satan has knowledge concerning the future. When our Lord was on earth the demons cried out "What have we to do with thee, Jesus, thou Son of God? Art thou come hither to torment us before the time?" (Matt. viii:29). From this we learn that the demons know the difference between the first and second coming of our Lord. They know when He comes the second time their doom will be sealed and they will no longer be permitted to torment and ruin the bodies and souls of men. Satan unquestionably knows his doom and that it is linked up with the Return of our Lord. He also knows that the church, as the body of Christ, must be completed before He comes again. This must be a leading reason why he hates the church and attempts to corrupt it by evil doctrines and persecutes those who are Christ's. All his efforts are unavailing for the Lord Jesus Christ keeps His people.

World Dominion Satan's Endeavor

Throughout this age this enemy of God also endeavors to control the earth politically and rule the nations. The Roman emperors mostly all aimed at world-dominion and did the devil's bidding to obtain their object. What horrible things were done and the depths of wickedness history makes known to us. Throughout the centuries of our age, again and again, he raised up instruments and inspired them to great deeds in bloody wars to control nations and kingdoms. Napoleon is a notable example. His ambition was to become the head of a great European empire. A cartoonist of 1812 pictured Satan holding Napoleon in his lap and saying to him, "This is my beloved son in whom I am well pleased." If this was true of Napoleon that he was of the seed of the serpent, doing his will, how much more is it true of the Hohenzollern, William II. His deeds and the deeds of his associates in this war of all wars surpass the deeds of Nero, Attila and Napoleon. The devil's bait was swallowed by this Prussian emperor and he hoped to gain world dominion, but has now found out that the devil is a liar.

Nor must we forget the popes with their spurious claims of being Christ's vice-regents on earth and their attempt to exercise temporal power. Behind their claim there stands the same dark shadow.

Satan's Final Opposition

When this age ends Satan will make a final effort in opposing God. He will be permitted to succeed for a brief time and do what is in his heart to do. This takes place after the true church has left the earth. Satan will then be cast out of heaven and coming down to this earth once more in person, he manifests great wrath, knowing that he hath but a short time (Rev. xii:12).[5] The mystery of lawlessness, which has been at work from the beginning will break out fully and find a consummation through the power of Satan. The thirteenth chapter of Revelation gives the future history of Satan's seeming success and triumph. He will succeed in forming a great empire, which is the old Roman empire in a revived form. This empire, which is called a beast, will receive Satan's power, and will have over it a wicked leader, whom Daniel saw as the little horn on the ten-horned beast.[6] The dragon's plan to control the earth has seemingly been realized. He then institutes the great tribulation. But there is a second beast mentioned in Revelation xiii. He has two horns like a lamb but speaks as a dragon. This is the Antichrist, the man of sin, the son of perdition. Like the little horn, the political leader, this second beast is Satan's man. He leads the religious apostasy and tries to stamp out what is left of the truth of God on the earth. He himself claims to be God and takes the place in the temple of God (in Jerusalem), and by lying signs and wonders backs up his claims. His work is described in Rev. xiii:11-18 and 2 Thess. ii:3-12. Fearful will be those days when the true church is gone and when God, as a judgment, lets Satan rule over those who rejected the offers of His love in His blessed Son. Another work of his is seen in the final Babylon and the scarlet clad woman, who rides the beast (the revived Roman empire). And finally when the hour approaches of Christ's visible and glorious return, Satan summons "the kings of the earth and their armies, gathering them together to make war against Him that sat on the horse and against his army" (Rev. xix:19). But then his defeat has come. The King of kings and Lord of lords appears in glory. The glory-flash, the brightness of His Coming strikes down the beast and the false prophet (Antichrist). The battle of Armageddon of short duration is over. Satan and all his hosts are utterly defeated. In Revelation xx we have the record of what will happen to the dragon, that old serpent, which is the Devil and Satan. He will be chained and cast into the pit of the abyss for a thousand years so that he can seduce the nations no more. He is dethroned and Christ is enthroned. Christ and His Saints reign over the earth. During this millennium righteousness and peace will reign. Wars will be no more, for the supreme war-lord is chained in prison. Armies will be unknown, for he who is behind it all has no more power. Idolatries and its degrading immoralities are no longer known, for he who deceived the nations has been arrested. Nor will there be any more cults which deny the Lord, His virgin birth, His resurrection, for the liar can lie no more and the visible presence of Christ stops every mouth.

After this millennium of indescribable blessing and glory, Satan will be permitted to get out of the prison for a little season.[7] His first work is to begin another war encompassing the camp of the Saints. A swift judgment follows. "And the devil that deceived them was cast into the lake of fire and brimstone, where the beast and the false prophets are, and shall be tormented day and night for ever and ever" (Rev. xx:10). His eternal dwelling place will be the lake of fire, not to be destroyed, but to live on forever and ever. There too will be the beast and the false prophet and all who are not found written in the book of life. (Rev. xx:15).

And then what? "And I saw a new heaven and a new earth, for the first heaven and the first earth were passed away and there was no more sea. And John saw the holy city, new Jerusalem, coming down from God out of heaven, prepared as a bride for her husband. And I heard a great voice out of heaven saying, Behold the tabernacle of God is with men, and He will dwell with them, and they shall be His people, and God himself shall be with them, and be their God. And God shall wipe away all tears from their eyes; and there shall be no more death, neither sorrow, nor crying, neither shall there be any more pain, for the former things are passed away" (Rev. xxi:1-4).

Such is the history of Satan. It is the history of the earth, and a marvellous history it is.

The original earth, once Satan's domain, then judged and covered by water and darkness on account of his revolt. The earth as it is now is given to man and Satan through the fall of man laying hold of it again. Then the long history of the conflict for well nigh 6,000 years. The Son of God, the Creator of all things, appearing on earth to procure the needed redemption; Satan defeated every step of the way. And after Satan's power manifested to the full, Christ appears and rids this earth,

71

for whose redemption He paid by His blood, of the dark shadow. And finally this earth becomes in its eternal state, as a new earth, surrounded by a new heaven, the eternal dwelling place of God in the midst of His redeemed people.

[1] The question may be asked by some, "If Satan and his angels possessed the earth and were dispossessed, to what other place did they go?" Undoubtedly the atmosphere surrounding this earth, called the first heaven. Satan is called "The prince of the power of the air" (Eph. ii:2). Notice also the work of putting the firmament in order, the atmosphere, on the second day (Gen. i:7) is not pronounced good.

[2] Cain in rejecting God's way of approach by sacrifice and bringing instead his own works was the first Unitarian and Christian Scientist.

[3] See "The Present Age" in this volume.

[4] "Exposition of Revelation," by A. C. Gaebelein, unfolds this more fully.

[5] See chapter "The Redemption of the Purchased Possession."

[6] The Roman Empire in its final form of ten kingdoms.

[7] See "Revelation," by A. C. Gaebelein, in explanation of this interesting prophecy.

THE CONVERSION OF THE WORLD AND THE JEWS

The term, the conversion of the world, is nowhere used in the Bible. That there is, according to the predictions of God's Holy Word, a wonderful future in store for the earth, when nations will learn war no more, but learn righteousness instead, and worship Jehovah as King and Lord, is too well known to every intelligent Christian to need restatement. When that jubilee time comes the knowledge of the glory of the Lord will cover the earth as the waters cover the deep; the groaning creation, now so sadly sharing in the curse of man's sin, will be delivered from its groans. It is noteworthy that there are no promises in the New Testament which would authorize the Church of God to expect the accomplishment of these predictions as the result of her testimony and activity. If this were her work, to convert the world, to lead nations to know God, to abandon the most horrible result of sin, war—we would have to confess that she has failed miserably. Nor is it true, as some now say, that this world war will, when it ends, bring about these blessed things by man's renewed efforts. If it is the work of present agencies, the expected world conversion lies in an unreachable distance.

According to Prophecy

It is in the Old Testament Prophetic Word where we find the promises that the nations of the world will be brought to know God, that all the ends of the earth shall turn to the Lord and that all kings shall fall down before Him. It is written that "All nations shall serve Him," "All nations shall call Him blessed," and that the whole earth will be filled with His glory.[1] Nor is the Old Testament Prophetic Word silent as to how and when all this is to be brought about. As the writer has shown in his "Harmony of the Prophetic Word," before this glorious future can come for the nations of the earth the Lord's return must have taken place; and this event is preceded by judgments upon the nations, and partial restoration of God's ancient people to their own land, the calling of a God-fearing remnant amongst them, and by the great Tribulation. When these things have come to pass, immediately after the days of that Tribulation, our Lord will appear in the clouds of Heaven with power and great glory. The Day of Vengeance has come, but in wrath mercy will be remembered. All Israel living in that day will be saved, and His Kingdom will be established upon this earth. The nations of the earth are then gathered into this kingdom. They will not be gathered into the Church, as is often said, for the Church is no longer here but has entered into glory to reign with Christ over the earth.

Daniel in his vision beheld the Son of Man coming with the clouds of Heaven: "And there was given Him dominion and glory, and a kingdom, that all people, nations and languages should serve Him. His dominion is an everlasting dominion which shall not pass away, and His kingdom that which shall not be destroyed" (Dan. vii:13-14). As the result of the first coming of our Lord in humiliation and His sacrificial death He receives the Church, which is now forming during this age. When He comes the second time He receives this world-wide Kingdom, in which the nations of the earth will be subjects. When that time comes, and not before, the kingdoms of this world become the Kingdom of our Lord and of His Christ, "and He shall reign forever and ever" (Rev. ii:15). So much for the conversion of the world, and the blessings promised to the nations and to the whole earth. It is inseparably linked with the second coming of Christ.

The Nations which Enter into the Kingdom

In Matthew xxv:31 our Lord speaks of what will take place when He has returned, "When the Son of Man shall come in His glory, and all the holy angels with Him, then shall He sit upon the throne of His glory, and before Him shall be gathered all nations, and He shall separate them one from another as a shepherd divideth his sheep from the goats; and He shall set the sheep on His right hand, but the goats on the left." We are aware that this passage is often looked upon as teaching a universal judgment of the whole human race; but it is not that. Not a word is said by our Lord concerning the resurrection of the dead. The dead are not included in this judgment. This judgment can therefore not be identified with the Great White Throne Judgment of Revelation xx. Nor is the Church in any way connected with this judgment, because when that takes place the saints are with the Lord in glory. It is the judgment of the living nations which the Lord finds on earth at the time of His second coming. This judgment will cover the first part of His reign as King, when He will first rule like David in subduing His enemies, when Gog and Magog, under the leadership of the Prince of Rosh, will also be dealt with in judgment (Ezekiel xxxviii and xxxix), and that will be followed by His reign as Prince of Peace, as foreshadowed by the reign of Solomon. Now, at this judgment of the nations, when He divides them as a shepherd divideth his sheep from the goats, there will be nations which He puts at His right hand, and to which He saith, "Come ye blessed of My Father, inherit the kingdom prepared for you from the foundation of the world." These nations are therefore converted nations, righteous nations, declared to be fit for that Kingdom over which He will reign. The question arises, When were these nations converted? Though the Gospel has been preached for about 1900 years yet we do not know of any converted nation on the earth to-day. The nations which we term Christian nations are at present engaged in the most bloody war of all history. Yet in as much as the Lord finds converted nations on the earth when He comes back and receives His throne, these nations must have been converted previous to His coming. It is therefore an important and interesting question, When and how were the nations converted which the Lord at the judgment of nations calls blessed, and bids to enter the Kingdom on earth? They were not converted by the preaching of the Gospel as it is done to-day, for if they were converted as the result of the testimony of the Church they would share in the glorious destiny, "Caught up in clouds to meet the Lord in the air." The only alternative then is that they will be converted after the true Church has been completed and taken into glory.

Sometimes before our Lord is manifested from Heaven with His holy angels, a turning of nations to God must therefore take place. It will be during the time when God deals with this earth in mighty judgments, when the earth and the heavens are shaken, when Antichrist, Satan's masterpiece, is on the earth and produces the Great Tribulation. It will be one of the startling events of the end of the age, after the Church has been removed from the earth. During these years of trouble, judgment, and great tribulation, God will give a final witness to all nations. Of this our Lord speaks in Matt. xxiv:14, "And this Gospel of the Kingdom shall be preached in all the world for a witness unto all nations, and then shall the end come." Though the Gospel of Grace is being preached world-wide, the preaching of the Gospel of the Kingdom as a witness unto all nations has not yet taken place. It falls into the seven years preceding the visible coming of our Lord.

Who Will be Used in the Conversion of These Nations?

But who will be the preachers who proclaim the Gospel of the Kingdom if all true Christians have left the earth and the true Church is no longer here? The apostates and destructive critics of to-day, with the mass of professing Christians who received not the love of the Truth will surely not take up the preaching of the Gospel of the Kingdom, for we read in the Word of God that those who received not the love of the Truth that they might be saved will follow the strong delusion of Antichrist and believe the lie (2 Thess. ii:10-11). Who then are the preachers? An elect company of God's ancient people, Israel. They are now scattered among all the nations of the earth, judicial blindness is upon them; but it will not be always so, for God has not cast away His people.

When the Church is gone the Lord will not leave the world without a witness. He will raise up a company of God-fearing people, Israelites; take away the veil from their hearts and use them as heralds. As it was in the beginning of this present dispensation, so will it be at the close. The first preachers were Jews, and the last heralds before the Lord comes in visible glory will again be Jews. To them will be given the last evangel of God's mercy to a lost world. "To every nation, and kindred, and tongue, and people" (Rev. xiv:6); and the message, "Fear God and give glory to Him for the hour of His judgment is come, and worship Him that made heaven and earth, and the sea, and the fountains of waters" (Rev. xiv:7). They will preach the Gospel of the coming Kingdom, that the Kingdom is about to come, and then call upon all nations to repent and turn to God.

It would be intensely interesting if we could follow the calling of this remnant of Israelites for this testimony as revealed in different portions of the Old Testament. Such a remnant of believing Israelites is anticipated in the Psalms, which speak of the coming final deliverance of Israel. There we read of their persecutions, their prayers, and their

75

expectations. The reader will please turn to Psalm xliv:10-26; Psalms lv to lvii; Psalm lxiv, lxxix and lxxx; Isa. lxiii:15 to Isa. lxiv. And how well this remnant is fitted to give a world-wide testimony among all nations, for they are scattered amongst the nations and acquainted with the different languages. Therefore the preaching of the Gospel of the Kingdom to all nations will be accomplished before the real end comes.

Revelation—Chapter Seven

We call attention here to the seventh chapter of Revelation. In this chapter we read of the sealing of one hundred and forty-four thousand. How much confusion might have been avoided if expositors and Christians had not lost sight of two facts in connection with this sealed company. First, this sealed company cannot be called now, nor are they in connection with the Church of God, because the Church according to the scope of the Book of Revelation is no longer on the earth when this takes place; and secondly, the Word states clearly that these sealed ones are "of all the tribes of the children of Israel." This sealed company therefore is of Israel, and will be called after the Church has been removed to her heavenly destination.

In the second half of this chapter in Revelation we read of another company. John writes, "After this I beheld, and lo, a great multitude, which no man could number, of all nations and kindreds, and people, and tongues, stood before the throne, and before the Lamb, clothed with white robes and palms in their hands." When one of the elders had asked, "Who are these which are arrayed in white robes, and whence came they?" He told John, "These are they which came out of the Great Tribulation and have washed their robes and made them white in the blood of the Lamb." We learn that this multitude of all nations comes out of the Great Tribulation. It is not the Church, for the Church is not in the Great Tribulation. This great multitude represents the Gentile nations who heard the final testimony and who believed, They turned in repentance to God and were then washed in the Blood of the Lamb. This great company does not stand before a heavenly throne, but it is the millennial throne which is in view here, and their blessedness throughout the millennial kingdom, after having suffered in the Great Tribulation, is described. They are the nations which the King calls blessed, and which will inherit the Kingdom. They are the fruits of the faithful witness of the elect Jewish remnant heralding the Kingdom before the Lord comes.

"These My Brethren"

When our Lord addresses from His throne these converted nations He says, "Inasmuch as ye have done it unto one of the least of these my brethren, ye have done it unto Me." Who are His brethren? He means by this term His brethren according to the flesh, from whom as concerning the flesh He came (Rom. ix:4-5). The nations who listened to their testimony when they appeared with the Gospel of the Kingdom, and who believed that message, manifested their belief by treating the messengers with kindness, giving them to eat and to drink, and clothing them. They did what the Gentile Rahab did to the Jewish spies, the advanceguard of the victorious host of Israel. And the other nations who despised the final offer of God's mercy in the preaching of the Gospel of the Kingdom showed no kindness to the Jewish messengers; and these nations which spurned the last offer will pass away from the earth.

What Else Converted Israel Will Do

When the Lord comes all Israel living in that day will be saved, except the apostates (Ezekiel xx:38), those who have worshipped the Beast and followed Anti-christ. "They shall look upon Him Whom they have pierced, and mourn for Him" (Zech. xii:10). This converted nation will be a kingdom of priests, and become the nucleus of that Kingdom into which the nations converted during the Tribulation, and all nations throughout the Millennium, will be gathered. Beautiful are the words of Isaiah, speaking of that time (Isa. lxi:6-9): Then the Gentiles shall come to the light which has risen among that nation, and kings to their brightness. Read the sixtieth chapter of Isaiah. In fact the entire prophetic Word witnesses to the fact that Israel, so long a curse among the nations, will be a blessing to all the nations.

It seems from another passage that when the Millennium begins with the coming of the King, that certain portions of the earth must yet be reached, and that work is to be done among different nations to make known the great events which have taken place. And God will use Israel for this work. Isa. lxvi:19: "And I will set a sign among them, and I will send those that escape of them unto the nations, to Tarshish, Pul, and Lud, that draw the bow, to Tubal, and Javan, to the isles afar off, that have not heard my fame, neither have seen my glory; and they shall declare my glory among the Gentiles." The last sentence of this prophecy, "they shall declare my glory among the Gentiles," tells us that they will have a work to do after His glory has been manifested. There is another passage in Zechariah which also speaks of how they will be used, Zech. viii:23: "Thus saith the Lord of hosts: In those days it shall come to pass, that ten men shall take hold out of all languages of the nations, even shall take hold of the skirt of him that is a Jew saying, We will go with you, for we have heard that God is with you." This necessarily also comes after the Lord has come and set up His Kingdom.

Israel will therefore be definitely used in bringing the nations of the earth into the Kingdom. In that coming Kingdom, converted, Spirit-filled Israel will be the head of all nations, and be used in world-wide ministry and blessing. Then will be fulfilled what the Lord said through Isaiah: "Ye shall be named the priests of the Lord; men shall call you ministers of our God; ye shall eat the wealth of the nations, and in their glory shall ye boast yourselves." What blessing is in store for the whole world, when that time comes may also be learned from Rom. xi:12-15. Let all true believers pray as never before, "Even so, come Lord Jesus."

[1] We give a few of the many passages which predict these things. Read them carefully with the contex: Psalm xxii:27-28, xlvii:7-8, lxvii:4-5, lxxii; Isa. lx:2-9; Dan. vii:13-14; Zech. ii:11.

THE FEASTS AND THE NAMES

Leviticus xxiii

The Lord commanded His people Israel to keep seven yearly feasts. We find them mentioned in their proper order in Leviticus. The feasts, or holy convocations are: The Feast of Passover, the Feast of Unleavened Bread, the Feast of First-fruits, the Feast of Pentecost, the Feast of Trumpets, the Day of Atonement and the Feast of Tabernacles. While these feasts had a special meaning for God's people Israel and their worship they are also "the shadow of things to come;" they have a decided prophetic meaning. In a most remarkable manner they reveal the whole plan of redemption. All the dispensational dealings of God with Jews and Gentiles may be traced in these feasts.

We find also in the Old Testament Scriptures seven compound names of Jehovah. These are the following: *Jehovah-Jireh* (Jehovah provides), Gen. xxii:14; *Jehovah-Rophekah* (Jehovah thy Healer), Exod. xv:26; *Jehovah-Nissi* (Jehovah my banner), Ex. xvii; *Jehovah-Shalom* (Jehovah is Peace), Judges vi:24; *Jehovah-Roi* (Jehovah my Shepherd), Psalm xxiii:1; *Jehovah-Tsidkenu* (Jehovah our Righteousness), Jer. xxiii:6; *Jehovah-Shammah* (Jehovah is there), Exek. xlviii:35. These names are also prophetic; they tell out the story of redemption and may be linked with the Feasts of Jehovah. The interesting fact is that these names are given in the Word in such an order that they correspond with these feasts of Jehovah.

I. The Passover Feast. This was to be observed on the fourteenth day of the month of Abib and was kept in memory of Israel's redemption and deliverance from Egypt, the house of bondage. The Passover-lamb was slain and its blood sprinkled on the lintel and side-posts of the door. God assured them when they were in Egypt, "When I see the blood I will pass over you." And so it was. The blood of the slain lamb sheltered them and secured immunity from death. The lamb, as a spotless victim, died that they might live. This feast marked the beginning of Israel's history as a redeemed people; their years were to be counted from that day (Exod. xii:1). The blessed story of this great redemption was not to be forgotten, but to be remembered from generation to generation (Exod. xii:24-27). The Passover lamb and the sheltering blood foreshadow most blessedly the atoning work of the Cross, the sacrifice of our Lord and His precious blood. The paschal lamb is a type of Christ our Passover. "Christ our Passover is sacrificed for us" (1 Cor. v:7). Our Lord fulfilled the type in every detail. When the time came for the Lord Jesus Christ to give His life, Satan made an effort that His death should not occur on the Passover-feast. Satan knew that he was the true Lamb, and so he tried to prevent His death at the proper time (Matt. xxvi:5; Mark xiv:2). But the Lamb of God died at the very time, thus fulfilling the Scriptures. Redemption by blood stands first, for it is the foundation of everything.

Jehovah-Jireh—"the Lord will provide"—is His name in connection with Abraham when he put his son Isaac as a sacrifice upon the altar. When Isaac asked, "Where is the lamb for a burnt-offering?" Abraham answered, "My son, God will Himself provide the lamb for a burnt-offering" (Gen. xxii:8). The ram was provided to be put upon the altar and Abraham called the place Jehovah-Jireh. And so the Lord has provided the Lamb; He has provided a free and full salvation through His own Son. How beautifully this name of Jehovah fits the Passover feast needs not to be demonstrated. Every one can see this.

II. The Feast of Unleavened Bread. This feast could not be separated from Passover. Passover without the feast of unleavened bread would have not only been an impossibility, but an insult to God. And so also the feast of unleavened bread without the Passover. Leaven is always the type of evil, corruption and sin. An unleavened condition means the opposite, it means holiness. God redeems unto holiness. What He redeems is destined to share His own holy character. This feast of unleavened bread was to be kept for seven days. In Corinthians (1 Cor. v:7-8), where we read of Christ our Passover, the unleavened bread is likewise mentioned. "Christ our Passover is sacrificed for us; wherefore let us keep the feast, not with old leaven, neither with the leaven of malice and wickedness but with the unleavened bread of sincerity and truth." And before this it is written "Know ye not that a little leaven leaveneth the whole lump? Purge out, therefore, the old leaven, that ye may be a new lump, as ye are unleavened." Redemption delivers from the power of indwelling sin. Redeemed by blood, and saved by grace, our calling is unto holiness. Spiritually to keep the feast of unleavened bread means to live in the energy of the new nature, walking in the Spirit. And ultimately His redeemed people will be wholly sanctified delivered from the very presence of sin. He will present the church to Himself, "a glorious church, not having spot, or wrinkle, or any such thing; but that it should be holy and without blemish" (Eph. v:27). That will be when we shall be with Him in glory. Then the gracious work of redemption is completed and crowned.

Jehovah-Rophekah, "the Lord thy Healer," He calls Himself in Exod. xv:26. "Bless the Lord, O my soul, and forget not all His benefits; who forgiveth all thine iniquities, who healeth all thy diseases, who redeemeth thy life from destruction, who crowneth thee with loving kindness and tender mercies" (Psalm ciii:2-4). We look forward to the day when in the kingdom to come "the inhabitant shall not say, I am sick" (Isa. xxxiii:24), when His redeemed, blood-washed people shall be glorified and then wholly sanctified as to body, soul and spirit. When our body of humiliation is changed that it may be fashioned like unto His glorious body (Phil. iii:21), then shall we know all the gracious power of Jehovah-Rophekah.

III. The Feast of First-fruits. The third feast is the Feast of First-fruits (Lev. xxiii:9-14). While the Passover typifies the death of Christ, the waving of the sheaf of the first fruits is the blessed type of the physical resurrection of our Lord Jesus Christ. It is the third feast; the number three in the Word of God is almost in every instance connected with resurrection. One sheaf only was brought into the presence of Jehovah; this sheaf was the earnest of the harvest to follow. "But now is Christ risen from the dead, and become the first-fruits of them that slept" (1 Cor. xv:20). "But every man in his own order: Christ, the first-fruits; afterward they that are Christ's at His Coming" (1 Cor. xv:23). The grain of wheat had fallen into the ground and died. But He liveth; the full ear of the sheaf waved before Jehovah typifies the abundant fruit which He brings unto God. It was waved "on the morrow after the Sabbath." That is the first day of the week, the glorious resurrection morning. Thus we see in this feast Christ risen from the dead, the first-fruits, now at the fight hand of God. And as He was raised from among the dead, so shall His people be raised from among the dead, when He descends from heaven with the shout; while living believers shall be changed in a moment. And all will be with Him in that blessed day when He comes for His own.

Jehovah-Nissi, "the Lord my Banner" (Exod. xvii:15). Israel, as we read in this chapter, fought with Amalek (the type of the flesh). Joshua was the leader of God's people in this warfare, while Moses was on the top of the hill holding up his hands that Israel might prevail. And Joshua gained the victory over Amalek. Joshua typifies Christ risen from the dead, who, like Joshua, brings His people through Jordan into the promised land. And Moses on the top of the hill with his uplifted hands also represents Christ risen from the dead, at God's right hand interceding for His people. Through a risen Christ, whose life we have, and who liveth for us, we get the victory in the conflict down here. He died for us, which gives us peace; He lives for us and in us, which gives us power. The risen Christ is our banner and victory.

IV. The Feast of Pentecost (verses 15-22). This is the Feast of Weeks, also called Pentecost (the Greek word for fifty) because it was celebrated fifty days after the Feast of First-fruits. After seven Sabbaths had passed by, a new Meal-offering was to be brought to the Lord. It consisted of two loaves, which were of fine flour, leaven also was to be put in them; they were to be the first-fruits unto the Lord. In the beginning of Leviticus we read of the meal-offering. The offering here in the Feast of Weeks, or Pentecost, was a new meal-offering. The meal-offering in the first part of this book (ii:1-16) is the type of Christ in His perfect humanity. In that meal-offering there was no leaven, but fine flour was mixed with oil, and oil was poured upon it before it was exposed to the fire. All this blessedly foreshadows the Lord Jesus in His spotless humanity and the sufferings through which He passed. But here is a new meal-offering, into which leaven was put.

Fifty days after Christ arose, when the day of Pentecost had come, the Holy Spirit descended out of heaven. While He filled the assembled believers in Jerusalem, He also baptized them into one body; the church, the body of Christ, began with this great event. The new meal-offering, therefore, is a prophetic type of the church. Let us notice that the loaves of this new meal-offering were also called "first-fruits." This word identifies them with Him who is the first-fruits of them that slept, the Lord Jesus Christ. He is the First-fruits and His believing people are likewise called by that name. "Of His own will begat He us with the word of truth, that we should be a kind of first-fruits of His creatures" (Jas. i:18). Believers have the first-fruits of the Spirit (Rom. viii:23). Christ also is the firstborn, while believers are His brethren destined to share His glory (Rom. viii:29); and the church is called the church of the firstborn" (Heb. xii:23).

This new meal-offering, a type of the church, was made of fine flour, which comes from the corn of wheat. It typifies the true believer, who is born again, and possesses the new nature, and only those who are born again are members of the true church. The leaven put into this offering is the type of sin and the old nature, which is still in the believer. Therefore the sin-offering was made prominent in connection with this feast, which tells us of the blessed work of Christ as the sin-bearer of His people. The two loaves foreshadow believing Jews and Gentiles, which compose the church. Some day the church will be presented to the Lord, as the new meal-offering was brought into His presence. This will happen when the Lord comes for His Saints.

Jehovah-Shalom, "the Lord is Peace" (Judges vi:24). How beautifully this name of Jehovah harmonizes with Pentecost. He has made peace in the blood of the Cross. "Peace be unto you" was His blessed word of greeting to the assembled disciples on the resurrection day. And ever since He is in the midst of those who gather unto His Name and His blessed, precious word of peace remains throughout this age for His redeemed people. Furthermore, "He is our peace, who hath made both one, and hath broken down the middle wall of partition, having abolished in His flesh the enmity, the law of commandments in ordinances, for to make in Himself of twain one new man, so making peace. And that He might reconcile both unto God, in one body by the cross having slain the enmity thereby. And came and preached peace to you which were far off, and to them that were nigh" (Ephes. ii:14-17).

But let us notice here that four months elapsed before another feast was kept. During these four months the harvest and vintage took place. The feast of Pentecost had after it this long period before the trumpet was blown for another solemn feast. This interval has a prophetic meaning of much importance. Dispensationally we are still in the Feast of Pentecost. This age is the age of Pentecost. The Holy Spirit is present to accomplish His great mission, which is to gather out the church. This blessed work goes on during this age. But some day the Spirit's work will surely be finished and the new meal-offering, the church, will be presented in glory. How this will be accomplished we know from 1 Thess. iv:13-18 and 1 Cor. xv:5 1-54.

Let us remember then that the four feasts foreshadow the Cross of Christ (Passover); the Work of the Cross which is complete Redemption (Unleavened Bread); the Resurrection of Christ (First-Fruits); the Holy Spirit and His Work on earth, the out-calling of the church (Pentecost). We are living in the interval between Pentecost and the fifth feast. But the next feast in its prophetic meaning will not come till the church is completed and presented unto the Lord. The harvest has to come. And the harvest is in verse 22 the same as in Matt. xiii:39.

Recently a theory has been advanced according to which the Lord must come for His Saints on the Jewish feast of Trumpets. But that is only a speculation. It is disproven by the fact that the new meal-offering on the feast of Pentecost, typifying the church, must be first presented to the Lord, before the feast of trumpets can come. What the feast of trumpets foreshadows we shall see next.

V. The Feast of Trumpets. The feast of trumpets, the day of atonement and the feast of tabernacles in their prophetic meaning are still future. Nor will the events foreshadowed come to pass till the harvest, the end of the age, comes, and the church has been removed from the earth. The trumpets here must not be identified with the last trump in 1 Cor. xv:53 or the trump of God in 1 Thess. iv. The feast of trumpets does not foreshadow the Coming of the Lord for His Saints. The feast of trumpets shows prophetically the call of God to the remnant of His earthly people. They are to be regathered and a remnant of them is to be brought back. But the Lord does not regather earthly Israel as long as His heavenly people are still here. An awakening spiritually and nationally is predicted throughout the prophetic Word for His people Israel. See Isa. xxvii:13 and Joel ii:1. Matt. xxiv:31 has often been applied as meaning the church. This is incorrect. The elect to be gathered by the trumpets' sound is Israel. The blowing of the trumpets on the first day of the seventh month precedes the great day of atonement and heralds that approaching day.

Jehovah-Roi, "the Lord is my Shepherd" (Psalm xxiii:1). Christians have almost universally applied this precious Psalm to themselves and forgotten that Israel also has a part in it. He who is our Shepherd is the Shepherd of Israel. He gave His life as the good Shepherd for all His sheep; yea, He died for that nation (John xi:51). There is a day coming when this loving, caring Shepherd, who was here once and sought the lost sheep of the house of Israel, will seek them again. "Behold I, even I, will both search for my sheep and will seek them out. As a shepherd seeketh out his flock in the day that he is among his flock that are scattered, so will I seek out my sheep; and will deliver them out of all places whither they have been scattered in the day of clouds and thick darkness. And I will bring them out from the peoples and gather them from the countries, and will bring them to their own land, and feed them upon the mountains of Israel by the rivers and in all the inhabited places of the country" (Ezek. xxxiv:11-14). And when He gathers them, then will they joyfully praise Him as their Shepherd and know Jehovah-Roi.

VI. The Day of Atonement. This solemn feast followed immediately the blowing of the trumpets. Lev. xvi gives us the full description of that important day. On that day the blood of a sacrificial animal was carried within the vail and sprinkled by the high-priest on the mercy seat. When the high-priest has done this and came out from the Holiest the second sacrificial animal, a goat, was brought before him. He then put his hands upon the head of the goat and confessed upon it all the iniquities, the transgressions and sins of the children of Israel. "And the goat shall bear upon him all their iniquities unto a land not inhabited: and he shall let go the goat in the wilderness" (chapter xvi). And here the dispensational aspect comes in. Before the transgressions of Israel could be confessed over the scapegoat and before the goat could be sent forever away with its burden, the high-priest had to come out of the Holiest. As long as He remained alone in the Holiest, the goat could not carry away the sins of the people. When the Lord appears the second time, when He comes from heaven's glory as the King-Priest, then the blessed effect of His death for the nation will be realized and their sins and transgressions will forever be put away. Then they will in true repentance look upon Him whom they pierced and mourn for Him. And their sins will be forgiven and remembered no more. They will, through grace, become the righteous, the holy, the Spirit filled nation. "In that day there shall be a fountain opened to the house of David, and to the inhabitants of Jerusalem for sin and uncleanness" (Zech. xiii:1).

Jehovah-Tsidkenu—"The Lord our Righteousness." It is significant that this name of Jehovah appears twice in Jeremiah. Once it means our Lord and connected with the acknowledgement of Him as "our righteousness" is the promise that He shall reign as King. "In His days shall Judah be saved and Israel shall dwell safely, and this is His name whereby He shall be called 'Jehovah-Tsidkenu'" (Jer. xxiii:5-6). They will know Him as their righteousness, as we know Him as our righteousness. But when? When He has come and they accepted Him as their Lord and King. In Jer. xxxiii:16 the city of Jerusalem shall be called by that name. One of the future names of restored Jerusalem will be "the Lord our righteousness." No doubt, because the King has chosen her and manifests His glory in, round about and above Jerusalem.

VII. The Feast of Tabernacles. The seventh feast began on the fifteenth day of the seventh month and was kept after the harvesting. "Thou shalt observe the feast of Tabernacles seven days, after thou hast gathered in thy corn and thy wine" (Deut. xvi:13). Besides this it was a memorial feast of their wilderness journey of the past. Therefore they made booths of palm trees and willows. The palm is the emblem of victory and the willow the emblem of suffering and weeping. This feast is prophetic of the millennium and the coming glory, when Israel is back in the land and the kingdom has been established in their midst. Then the King will manifest Himself in the midst of His people. It will be a time of rejoicing and victory, when sorrow and sighing, so long the lot of Israel, will no more be heard. It comes after the harvest (the end of the age) and the vintage (the winepress of the wrath of God). The Gentiles, too, will join in that feast; it will be celebrated by Jews and Gentiles throughout millennial times (Zech. xiv:16), while the glorified church dwells with the Lord in the heavenly Jerusalem above the earth in marvellous glory, seen by the inhabitants of the world during the millennial age. It will probably be during that feast that the King of kings and Lord of lords will appear in visible glory in Jerusalem to receive the homage of Israel and the representatives of converted nations. How beautiful is the order of these last feasts of Jehovah! The blowing of the trumpets, the remnant of Israel called and gathered; the day of atonement, Israel in repentance, looking upon Him whom they pierced, when He comes the second time; the feast of Tabernacles, the Kingdom come, the time of peace and glory for the earth.

Jehovah-Shammah, "the Lord is there" (Exek. xlviii:35). The name of that city from that day shall be "Jehovah-Shammah"—the Lord is there. This is another millennial name of the city of Jerusalem. The closing chapters of Ezekiel tell us of Israel's restoration, the overthrow of their enemies, Gog and Magog, the powers from the North. Then the glory returns (Ezek. xliii:1-5), a wonderful temple is seen once more in Jerusalem, the Lord manifests Himself in the midst of the city and living waters will flow forth from Jerusalem. Thus the last compound name of Jehovah clearly points to millennial times.

We have seen that the feasts and the names of Jehovah are prophetic. They reveal the great redemption and tell us of the cross, the work accomplished there, how God made provision and redeems unto Himself. We traced in them His resurrection and the victory; the coming of the Holy Spirit, the formation and completion of the church; the regathering and the restoration of Israel, their spiritual blessing and the millennium. His Name is blessedly linked with these feasts. How wonderful is the blessed Word of God! And how we may find His gracious purposes in every portion of this Book of books. Soon the last three feasts may be ushered in. Let us therefore as His heavenly people, with a heavenly hope and destiny, wait daily for the promised home-call, the gathering shout.

"WHEN THE SHADOWS FLEE AWAY"

"Until the day break and the shadows flee away, I will get me to the mountain of myrrh, and to the hill of frankincense" (Sol. Song iv:6).

For nearly 6,000 years the shadows of sin and death and all which goes with it have been upon the human race. It has been a long and dreary night. Nor has that night become less as centuries passed by. Never before have the shadows of the night, the shadows of sin, been so dark and horrifying as now. Never before has there been so much sorrow, so much weeping and suffering in the earth as during our generation. That it will not be always so God's holy Word assures us. The night will end some day. "Watchman what of the night? Watchman, what of the night? The morning cometh." What morning did the watchman mean? It is that morning which all the great prophets of God beheld in holy vision. The morning when the day breaks and the shadows flee away. Then that which has been shall be again and peace on earth as well as glory to God in the highest will follow.

How and when will that long-promised morning come? Not through man's efforts. Not even through the preaching of the Gospel or the activities of the church. Not through a progressive civilization or through great reforms. Many expect in our days a better time for this earth as the result of the great struggle of nations. One of the slogans has been; "We fight to make the earth a decent place to live in;" while others believe that after the war a perfect and permanent peace with world-wide brotherhood and prosperity will solve all the problems of the human race. The complete overthrow of autocracy with its horrible crimes is in sight. Democracy will be victorious. Nations, we doubt not, will be brought together in a great league of nations, and all we have been fighting for as a nation to maintain justice and righteousness will be accomplished. But is this going to end sin? Will this mean that all the world turns now to God and to His Son? Will this victory end human suffering and wipe away all tears?

Will it bring back the lost paradise? Will famines and pestilences, earthquakes now be stopped? Will as a result of the victory of democracy groaning creation be delivered from its groans by the removal of the curse which has rested upon it so long? Has the perfect day come when all strife ceases forever and the sword can never again be unsheathed?

With all the achievements of our times and the realization of our human hopes the age is still "this present evil age," Satan is not yet dethroned, but he is still the ruler and the god of the age. The night is still on. The promised daybreak has not yet come when the shadows flee away. May

86

God's people remember this now when a wave of optimism no doubt will soon sweep this world, when everywhere the message of "peace and safety" will be preached, when the rush for world betterment will become almost irresistible.

Not Till He Comes

Not till the Lord Jesus Christ comes again and is enthroned as King over this earth will that day break when the shadows flee away. He alone can bring that longed for better day for the earth. His is the power and the glory to do it. He came from heaven down into this night of sin to purchase back His alienated creation. He paid the price so wonderfully great which only God can rightly value. The crown of thorns He wore because the thorns are the emblems of the curse which rests now upon creation as the result of man's sin. He tasted death for everything. On the cross He accomplished the mighty work, procured salvation for believing sinners, sealed Satan's doom, and that work is furthermore the pledge and guarantee of the victory for God in bringing back creation to its former perfect condition, only with greater glory added.

The once thorn-crowned Christ is in glory yonder. There faith's eye sees Him, who was made a little lower than the angels for the suffering of death crowned with glory and honor. But some day He will get the many crowns of which He is worthy, and when that glorious day comes, the shadows flee away.

"Come then, and, added to thy many crowns,
Receive yet one, the crown of all the earth,
Thou who alone art worthy! It was thine
By ancient covenant, ere Nature's birth;
And Thou hast made it thine by purchase since,
And overpaid its value with Thy blood."[1]

Let us see then what shadows will flee away when He comes back to earth again and claims His blood-bought inheritance. Let us see what glories are in store for this earth when the Son of Man receives that kingdom which will extend from sea to sea unto the uttermost parts of the earth.

I. As to His Redeemed People. The breaking of the day is heralded by the Morningstar, followed by the rising of the Sun in all his glory. Thus nature teaches us Scripture truths. Christ comes first for His own Saints; that is the Morningstar. And then He comes in fullest glory with all His

Saints as the sun of righteousness with healing in His wings; that is the sunrise when all shadows of the night will flee away.

The Saints of God wait now for the breaking of the day, for His coming as the Morningstar. And when He comes and opens with His triumphant shout the graves of the righteous dead, and calls the living Saints for the unspeakable change, in a moment, the twinkling of an eye, to put on immortality—then the shadows for His people are forever, yes forever, gone. No more bodies then of humiliation, but glorified bodies; no more separation from loved ones and from saints, but a blessed eternal reunion and fellowship; no more sorrow, but everlasting joy; no more crying and tears, but all tears wiped away; no more sinning, but perfect holiness; no more troubles, but perfect rest. What a glory time it will be when for us, His own beloved people the day breaks, and the shadows flee away. As shadows now increase, because the night is far spent and the day is at hand, the Saints of God should daily think of the soon coming day-break, that blessed, happy moment when we shall see Him as He is and shall be like Him.

II. The Shadows Will Flee Away from Israel and Israel's Land. No pen can describe the history of this people and the dark shadows which have been upon them. As the homeless nation they have wandered throughout this age, in fulfillment of the predictions of their own prophets, among the nations of the earth. Awful have been their persecutions, and tribulations upon tribulations have been their lot. Suffering and sorrow, the meat and drink of every generation since they were driven from their God-given land. How dark are the shadows which have come upon that people once more as the result of the world conflict. Millions have lost their all. Hundreds of thousands are homeless wanderers in eastern Europe. Perhaps the story of their suffering in connection with the war will never be written. And the end is not yet.

On the other hand their national hope has been revived as never before in their history. Regiments of Jews have gone forth into the war with their own flags, with David's shield in the center and the Hebrew word "Immanuel." They have been fighting like the Maccabees of old. Jerusalem has been captured from the Turks; all Palestine has passed into the hands of the Allies; never again can Turkey have dominion over the land she has so horribly misruled. What is to become of Palestine and Jerusalem? Let the answer be given through the letter which A. J. Balfour wrote in behalf of the British Government to Baron Rothschild: "The Government views with favor the establishment in Palestine of a national home for the Jewish people and will use their best endeavors to facilitate the achievement of this object, it being clearly understood that nothing will be done that may prejudice the civil or religious rights of existing non-Jewish communities in Palestine." Here is the answer of the French Government. "M. Sokolow, representing the Zionist organizations, was received by Monsieur Pichon, Minister for Foreign Affairs, who was happy to inform him that there is complete argeement between the French and English Governments in all matters which concern the establishment of a Jewish national home in Palestine." Our own country has fallen in line and pledged itself to see that at last the Jew is going to be treated with justice and that Palestine will become an independent Jewish state. No wonder there is great joy among the masses of Jews and that they too see a better day looming up for their people.

But do these tremendous events in the East mean that the day has come when the shadows flee away from the seed of Abraham? Not by any means. The time of Jacob's trouble has not yet been. The last siege of Jerusalem, prewritten in Zechariah's prophecy (chapter xiv) still awaits its fulfillment. To deliver that nation and that land completely and bring about the glories promised in God's infallible Word needs more than the conquest of the land. The flag of the British lion now flies over Jerusalem. Some day another flag will be raised above that city—the flag of the Son of Man, the Son of David, the Lion of the tribe of Judah.

Only when He comes again and His blessed feet stand once more upon the Mount of Olives, will that day of blessing and glory break for Israel with all shadows fleeing away. What it all will mean is fully written in prophecy. Much of what is written in the Book of Isaiah from chapter xl to the end of the vision of Isaiah refers to that glory time, when the King comes back, and when for Jerusalem the shadows flee away. Read especially chapters liv and lv; lxvi. In the other Prophets read the following chapters: Jeremiah xxx and xxxi; Ezekiel xxxiv-xlviii; Daniel vii:13-28 and chapter xii; Hosea iii:5, v:15, vi:1-3, xiv; Joel iii; Amos ix:11-15; Obadiah, verses 17-21; Micah iv-v; Habakkuk iii; Zephaniah iii:8-20; Haggai ii:6-9; Zechariah ii:6-13, viii, ix:9-11, xii-xiv. Here we have unfailing predictions of what will be when the day breaks and the shadows flee away from Israel.

III. The Shadows for All the Nations of the World Will Flee Away. In Revelation xx:3 we read that Satan, the Devil, that old Serpent is the deceiver of the nations. As we have seen in the lecture on the history of Satan he is the murder and liar from the beginning. He is responsible for every war which has ever been fought; he is the author of all idolatry; he blinds the nations and keeps them away from knowing God. For this reason peace cannot come till this dark shadow is chained, the world cannot be brought to God and do righteousness till this arch-deceiver is robbed of his power. We can rest assured that as long as this being is loose, world conversion and universal peace are unobtainable. And he will be chained by Him who is the strong One and has conquered him already—our Lord Jesus Christ. And therefore when He comes again the shadows will flee away from the nations of the earth. China will no longer be domineered over by demon influences; India, Africa and the islands of the sea will cast their idols away. All swords will become plowshares, all spears pruning hooks. Wars will cease even unto the ends of the earth; nations will learn war no more. The nations will learn righteousness; all oppression will cease; capital and labor has ended its strife; poverty is unknown; wickedness and crime of every description ends, for the King reigns in righteousness, and "in His day shall the righteous flourish and abundance of peace.... He shall have dominion also from sea to sea and from the river unto the ends of the earth.... all kings shall fall down before Him, all nations shall serve Him" (Psalm lxxii). Under His gracious reign of power famines and pestilences can no longer devastate this earth. Sickness and diseases will be banished and those who obey the laws of His kingdom will continue to live on earth, so that death, the common thing now, as the wages of sin, will become uncommon during the coming age. What a glory time there is in store for this earth! But we must not forget that day, when the shadows flee away, will be ushered in by a judgment of nations. Nations now in existence, steeped in unspeakable wickedness, having cast even a skin-deep civilization to the winds and outraged the laws of God and man, will be dealt with in judgment and pass away as nations (Matthew xxv:31).

IV. The Shadows which are upon Creation Will Also Flee Away. The Apostle Paul tells us of creation's curse, creation's groans and creation's deliverance: "For the earnest expectation of the creature waiteth for the manifestation of the sons of God. For the creature was made subject to vanity, not willingly, but by reason of him who hath subjected the same in hope. Because the creature itself also shall be delivered from the bondage of corruption into the glorious liberty of the children of God. For we know that the whole creation groaneth and travaileth in pain together until now" (Romans viii:19-22). Creation has fallen under the curse through man's sin. As man has continued in sin and has become worse in his deeds of defiance of God, creation has also seen degradation in a like degree. Blights are seen everywhere. Tidal waves and terrific earthquakes have destroyed human lives by the millions. All creation is suffering and groaning under the curse. But it is not to be so forever. The King who comes back is also the Creator, He who called all things into existence out of nothing. He surely will set all things in order and deliver groaning creation. He will put all things back as they were in the beginning and then earth will be once more a paradise. If He would do anything less than that the dark shadow of the one who brought sin

90

and death into the world would have the last word, and could then sneer into the face of God the fact that in spite of the redemption price He could not restore things as they were in the beginning.

We quote but one passage from the Book of Isaiah in which this blessed time is predicted when the shadows flee away for a groaning creation: "The wolf also shall dwell with the lamb, and the leopard shall lie down with the kid; and the calf and the young lion and the fatling together, and a little child shall lead them. And the cow and the bear shall feed; their young shall lie down together, and the lion shall eat straw like the ox. And the sucking child shall play at the hole of the asp, and the weaned child shall put his hand on the cockatrice den" (Isaiah xi:6-8). Do not say this has a spiritual meaning. It has not; it means what it says, and when the King comes back He will do it all in His mighty power.

"O scenes surpassing fables, and yet true,
Scenes of accomplish'd bliss! which who can see,
Though but in distant prospect, and not feel
His soul refreshed with foretaste of the joy?
Rivers of gladness water all the earth,
And clothe all climes with beauty; the reproach
Of barrenness is gone. The fruitful field
Laughs with abundance; and the land, once lean,
Or fertile only in its own disgrace,
Exults to see its thistly curse repeal'd;
The various seasons woven into one,
And that one season an eternal spring.
The garden fears no blight, and needs no fence,
For there is none to covet, all are full.
The lion, and the leopard and the bear
Graze with the fearless flocks; all bask at noon
Together, or all gambol in the shade
Of the same grove, and drink one common stream.
Apathies are none. No foe to man
Lurks in the serpent now; the mother sees
And smiles to see, her infant's playful hand
Stretch'd forth to dally with the crested worm,
To stroke his azure neck, or to receive
The lambent homage of his arrowy tongue.
All creatures worship man, and all mankind
One Lord, one Father. Error has no place;
That creeping pestilence is driven away;
The breath of heaven has chased it. In the heart
No passion touches a discordant string,

But all is harmony and love. Disease
Is not; the pure and uncontaminate blood
Holds its due course, nor fears the frost of age.
One song employs all nations; and all cry
'Worthy the Lamb, for He was slain for us!'"[2]

"Until the day break and the shadows flee away I will get me to the mountain of myrrh and to the hill of frankincense." The mountain of myrrh must mean the cross for myrrh means "bitterness" and was used in embalming the dead. As long as He tarries let God's people tent by His Cross and feast on His great love. And frankincense has the meaning of worship and praise. Let us worship and praise Him—"until the day break and the shadows flee away."

[1] William Cowper.
[2] William Cowper.

"FOR SOON SHALL BREAK THE DAY"

Up to the fair myrrh-mountain,
The fresh frankincense hill,
I'll get me in this midnight,
And drink of love my fill.
O hills of fragrance, smiling
With every flower of love;
O slopes of sweetness, breathing
Your odors from above!
Ye send me silent welcome,
I waft you mine again;
Give me the wings of morning,
Burst this still-binding chain;
For soon shall break the day,
And shadows flee away.

Amid time's angry uproar,
Unmoved, unruffled still,
Keep, keep me calmly, truly,
Doing the Loved One's will.
'Mid din of stormy voices,
The clamor and the war,
Keep me with eye full-gazing
On the eternal star;

Still working, suffering, loving,
Still true and self-denied,
In the old faith abiding,
To the old names allied;
For soon shall break the day,
And shadows flee away.

From earthly power and weakness
Keep me alike apart;
From self-will and unmeekness,
From pride of lip or heart.
Without let tempests gather;—
Let all be calm within,
Unfretted and unshaken
By human strife and sin.
And when these limbs are weary,
And throbs this sleepless brain,
With breath from yon myrrh-mountain
Revive my soul again;
For soon shall break the day,
And shadows flee away.

There my beloved dwelleth,
He calls me up to him;
He bids me quit these valleys,
These moorlands brown and dim.
There my long-parted wait me,
The missed and mourned below;
Now, eager to rejoin them,
I fain would rise and go.
Not long below we linger,
Not long we here shall sigh;
The hour of dew and dawning
Is hastening from on high;
For soon shall break the day,
And shadows flee away.

O streaks of happy day-spring
Salute us from above!
O never setting sunlight,
Earth longeth for thy love;
O hymns of unknown gladness,
That hail us from these skies,
Swell till you gently silence
Earth's meaner melodies!

O hope all hope surpassing,
For evermore to be,
O Christ, the Church's Bridegroom,
In Paradise with thee;
For soon shall break the day,
And shadows flee away.

THE COMING REIGN

King of kings! ascend Thy throne;
Visit this Thine earth again;
Gird Thy sword upon Thy thigh;
Take Thy mighty power, and reign

King of nations! claim this world
With its kingdoms for Thine own.
Raze each rebel fortress here,
Level every hostile throne.

King of Israel! now arise,
And rebuild Thy Salem's walls;
Gather Jacob's scattered flock;
Hear Thine Israel when he calls.

King of saints! Thy ransomed own,
They the members, Thou the head;
Speed the great deliverance,
First-begotten of the dead.

King of glory! King of heaven!
King of earth! arise and reign;
All creation sighs for Thee;
Visit Thine own earth again.

King eternal! Son of God!
Earth and heaven shall Thee obey;
Principalities and powers
Own Thine everlasting sway.

THESE ARE THE TRUE SAYINGS OF GOD

Sure the record; Christ has come!
Rich, for us became He poor.
O my soul, then know His love;
Love Him, serve Him evermore.

Sure the record; Christ has died,
Bearing on the cross our sin;

Is not this the gate of life?
Son of Adam, enter in!
  Sure the record; Christ is risen,
He hath broken every chain:
Silent stands the empty tomb,
Never to be filled again.
  Sure the promise; Christ will come,
Though the promise lingers still;
Heavy seems the wing of time,
Weary with the weight of ill.
  Signs are mustering everywhere,
And the world is growing old;
Love is low and faith is dull,
Truth and right are bought, and sold!
  Then when men are heedless grown,
And the virgins slumber all,
When iniquity abounds,
Then He cometh, Judge of all!
  Cometh He to raise His own
Wipe the tear from every eye;
Cometh He to right the wrong.
Trodden truth to lift on high.
  To dethrone the lie of lies,
Each dark falsehood to destroy;
To begin the age of light,
Earth's long sighed-for Sabbath-joy.

THE SUPPER AND THE ADVENT

  Till He come we own His name,
Round His table gathering;
One in love and faith and hope,
Waiting for an absent King.
Blessed table, where the Lord
Sets for us His choicest cheer;
Angels have no feast like this,
Angels wait, but sit not here.
  Till He come we eat this bread,
Seated round this heaven-spread board;
Till He come we meet and feast,
In remembrance of the Lord.
In the banquet house of love,

In the Bridegroom's garden fair;
Thus we sit and feast and praise,—
Angels look, but cannot share.

  Till He come we take this cup,—
Cup of blessing and of love;
Till He come we drink this wine,
Emblem of the wine above,—
Emblem of the blood once shed,
Blood of Him our sins who bare;
Angels look, but do not drink,
Angels never taste such fare.

  Till He come, beneath the shade
Of His love we sit and sing;
Over us His banner waves,
In His hall of banqueting.
Happy chamber, where the Lord
Spreads the feast with viands rare;
Angels now are looking on,
Angels serve, but cannot share.

  Till He come, we wear the badge
Of the ancient stranger-band;
Leaning on our pilgrim-staff,
Till we reach the glorious land.
Homeless here, like Him we love,
Watch we still in faith and prayer;
Angels have no watch like ours,
Angels have no cross to bear.

  Till He come, we fain would keep
These our robes of earth unsoiled;
Looking for the festal dress,
Raiment of the undefiled.
Ha! these robes of purest light,
Fairest still among the fair!
Angels gaze, but cannot claim,—
Angels no such raiment wear.

  Till He come we keep this feast,
Emblem of the feast above;
Marriage-supper of the Lamb,
Festival of joy and love.
Angels hear the bridal-song,
Angels set the festal fare;

Angels hear, but cannot join;
Angels wait, but cannot share.

CPSIA information can be obtained at www.ICGtesting.com
Printed in the USA
BVOW03s2252201014

371639BV00027B/600/P

9 781497 471429